THE BIRTH OF A MOTHER

ALSO BY DANIEL N. STERN, M.D.

The First Relationship (1977)

The Interpersonal World of the Infant (1985)

Diary of a Baby (1989)

The Motherhood Constellation (1995)

THE BIRTH OF A MOTHER

*How the Motherhood Experience
Changes You Forever*

Daniel N. Stern, M.D.,
and Nadia Bruschweiler-Stern, M.D.,

with Alison Freeland

BasicBooks
A Subsidiary of Perseus Books, L.L.C.

Grateful acknowledgment is made to Gail Greiner to reprint from "A Dangerous Thing to Hope For" © Gail Greiner, which appears in *Child of Mine,* edited and © 1997, Christina Baker Kline. Reprinted with permission by Hyperion.

Designed by Elliott Beard

Library of Congress Cataloging-in-Publication Data
Stern, Daniel N.
    The birth of a mother : how the motherhood experience changes you forever / by Daniel Stern.
       p.   cm.
    Includes bibliographical references and index.
    ISBN 0-465-01621-9
    1. Motherhood—Psychological aspects.   2. Mothers—Psychology.   I. Title.
HQ759.S689   1998
306.874'3—dc21   97-39533

98 99 00 01 02 ❖/RRD 10 9 8 7 6 5 4 3 2 1

To Adrien and Alice

Contents

CONTENTS

PART III

A Mother Adapts

Acknowledgments

W<small>E WISH,</small> above all, to acknowledge the many mothers who in their normal daily actions have inspired us, pointed out unseen directions, uncovered so many things that we were not fully aware of, and who simply taught us. In a similar vein, I (D.S.) am deeply grateful to my coauthor Nadia, and to Alison, for putting every part that I wrote through the crucial test of their experience as mothers.

Gail Winston, our editor, has been encouraging, critical, patient, and impatient, each at the right time in the needed dose. Her help has been immeasurable.

Some of the research and the writing of this book has been made possible thanks to support from the Steven Ross family.

THE BIRTH OF A MOTHER

INTRODUCTION

The Motherhood Mindset

THIS BOOK IS about the inner, often private experience of becoming a mother. In a sense, a mother has to be born psychologically much as her baby is born physically. What a woman gives birth to in her mind is not a new human being, but a new identity: the sense of being a mother. How does this identity emerge in each woman, and what does the process feel like? There are many books about the physiological and practical aspects of motherhood, but far less is written about the mental world where the new identity is formed. Becoming a mother is accomplished by the labor each woman performs on the landscape of her mind, labor resulting in a motherhood mindset, a deep and private realm of experience.

This motherhood mindset is not born at the moment the baby gives its first cry. The birth of a mother does not take place in one dramatic, defining moment, but gradually emerges from the cumulative work of the many months that precede and follow the actual birth of the baby.

What produces this motherhood mindset? How is it unique to each woman, yet shared by all mothers? What phases does it pass through? And how can you identify the passages of this remarkable new inner realm and learn to navigate its waters? That is the subject of this book.

We start at the beginning: Who exactly is a mother, and is she inherently different from other women? It may sound like a simple question, but in fact it strikes at the most basic assumptions held by the psychological and therapeutic communities.

As a psychiatrist, I have observed and treated parents and babies all my professional life. For almost thirty years, I researched the psychological development of infants, clinically observed the mother-infant relationship, and worked with mothers and babies whose relationships were disturbed. During most of that time, I considered a mother to be a woman with an added responsibility demanding new actions and reactions. True, she would have to develop a new repertoire of feelings and behaviors when she had a baby, but my conviction was that she would remain essentially the same woman she was before the baby was born.

Both male and female members of the psychological community have traditionally relied on accepted theories when working with mothers. Most psychological theories are based on general principles that apply to a broad spectrum of people and the ways their minds function. In the quest for general rules, psychotherapists have believed that all people have a basic psychic organization, or mindset, that explains their behavior. A person's mindset is thought to last a lifetime.

This mindset is what helps each one of us organize our mental lives. Our mindset determines what we consider most important, what we are most sensitive to, and what we notice in a given situation. It dictates what we find pleasant and exciting, frightening or boring. It affects the choices we make and our tendencies to act in one way instead of another. Our mindsets organize our mental lives to make us the coherent individuals we are.

Depending upon the orientation of a mental health professional, he or she will refer to an oedipal complex, or a secure or insecure personality, or a dependent or independent character, and use these theories to help a person understand his own mindset. No matter what theory is subscribed to, however, in none of them is motherhood viewed as anything but a slight variation on the already existing mindset. No one thought that a woman's mental life could fundamentally change with the arrival of a baby.

I believed this for many years until my coauthor (who is also my wife) helped me realize that the traditional psychological models did not accommodate the influence of motherhood on a woman's mindset. It was a simple realization, but it has profound implications for the mental health profession as well as for each woman entering the world of motherhood. In the course of becoming a mother, I realized, a woman develops a mindset fundamentally different from the one she held before, and enters a realm of experience not known to non-mothers. No matter what a woman's previous motives, vulnerabilities, and emotional reactions, when she becomes a mother, she will, for a time, operate from an entirely new mindset. This motherhood mindset pushes her preexisting mental life aside and rushes forward to fill the center stage of her inner life, giving it a different makeup entirely.

For me, the uniqueness of the motherhood mindset was a revelation, but in many ways it now seems almost to be simple common sense. After all, as you prepare to become a mother, you are facing an experience unlike any other in your life. When you have a baby, it will determine for a certain period of time what you think about, what you fear or hope for, and what your fantasies will be. It will influence your feelings and actions, and even heighten your basic sensory and information-processing systems. Having a child will redirect your preferences and pleasures, and most likely will realign some of your values. In a most startling way, it will influence all of your previous relationships, and cause you to reevaluate your closest associations and redefine your role in your own family's history.

As a mother, you will of necessity give birth to the motherhood mindset that for a time will act like the North Star in orienting your path in life. This is not merely a reorganization of your mental life, but an entirely new organization that will exist alongside (and most probably influence) your previous one. And all of this will happen inside your mind, while outside, in your physical life, you are learning to handle an equally new set of tasks such as feeding, nurturing, playing with, putting to sleep, and beginning to love this new human being. No wonder the mother's inner landscape has been little explored and explained. Mothers scarcely have time to identify it themselves!

As a mother hearing this for the first time, you may ask, "Is this mindset going to last my whole lifetime?" In my experience as a clinician, I see that it does last throughout a mother's life, but it does not always occupy center stage. After the birth of a baby, the motherhood mindset will fill the life of your mind, immediately determining your thoughts and behavior. Your previous mental organization is simply pushed into the background—for how long depends on the woman. It can dominate for several weeks, several months, or many years. Very often practical and financial realities such as the need to return to work play a large role in determining how long this mindset holds center stage.

As the practical realities of life demand more of your attention, the motherhood mindset will recede. However, the motherhood mindset in no way disappears, but rather waits in the wings, ready to come forward again whenever needed, such as when your child is sick, in trouble, or in danger. When your child needs you, you will react as a mother, no matter how old that child may be.

A television spot shown each night at ten o'clock on a New York City TV station for many years said, simply, "It is ten o'clock. Do you know where your children are?" I am convinced that at that moment, practically every mother hearing those words thought of her children, no matter if those children were forty weeks or forty years old. At that moment the motherhood mindset jumped forward to reclaim center stage, ready to go into action if necessary.

So in a deep and continuing way, the special mental organization that accompanies motherhood becomes a new and permanent part of you, to be used extensively at first, and then only at selected times. But its lasting presence, either in the foreground or background, makes you as a mother a unique kind of human being in ways that our existing psychological theories have failed to predict. You will never again be quite the same person you were before the baby, and while this shift should not be feared, neither should it be taken lightly. Consider some of the most dramatic changes in perspective.

THE SHIFT FROM DAUGHTER TO MOTHER

You have always been your mother's daughter, and this relationship, whether good or bad, has always been near the center of your identity. When you have a child, you begin to identify yourself primarily as a mother rather than as a daughter. Your life as someone's daughter becomes your past, just as your future as a mother begins, with all its grand possibilities.

With this basic change, which takes place over a short period of time, you may experience a profound loss as well as a wonderful gain. Either way, you will never again be simply a daughter. This shift in identity is responsible in part for the complex mix of emotions that most women feel following the birth of their babies. This explains why it is possible to feel happy and sad at once—happy about having a child and sad over what has been left behind.

TURNING TOWARD OTHER WOMEN

After you have a baby, you may be surprised by the way you perceive the people around you. You might find yourself becoming more interested in the community of women than you were in the past. Indeed, many new mothers become less concerned with men altogether. Most new mothers grow more curious about their own mother, for instance, and less about their father. You are likely to want to know more about how your mother was years ago as a mother to you, and less about how she is now either as a wife or a woman in her own right.

Most of our established psychological theories view a woman's relationship with other women, mothers included, in light of their relationships with men. For instance, when considering the interaction of two women, many psychologists will view the relationship as two points of a triangle, with the third point being a man, whether he is visible or not. This is another accepted theory that needs to change. At this time in a woman's life, when she has a new baby, it is more accurate to see her relationships with other women as standing independent of men.

SEEING YOUR HUSBAND DIFFERENTLY

So where, in this new community of women, does your husband fit in? Your perception of him will indeed be altered and you will probably find yourself more interested in his identity as a father to your baby than as a mate to you. Scientists can point to animal communities where this is true as well. A female baboon with a baby will allow a male into her life only if he proves himself a good caregiver to the youngster. You too will begin, consciously or unconsciously, to take your partner's abilities as a father into account as a key element in evaluating his attractiveness.

Husbands often find this shift hard to understand, particularly since it is often accompanied by a diminished desire for sex on the new mother's part. Hurt feelings and bruised egos can be avoided if husbands make an effort to learn the language and feelings associated with the motherhood mindset. It is important for them to understand that they are witnessing a natural and almost inevitable change shared by most new mothers and that it will be especially pronounced in the months immediately following the birth of the child.

For a time at least, there is a shift in emphasis when the normal dynamics having to do with sex, aggression, competition, and dominance are pushed more to the background, while caregiving, cooperation, nurturing, and creativity move to the foreground.

FORMING NEW TRIANGLES

It has long been thought that the triangle of mother, father, and child plays a central role in forming each of our personalities. Each of us is the product of such a triangle, and with the birth of our own child the triangle shifts down a generation. I propose, however, that a new and equally important psychological triangle starts to assume priority at this point. This new dynamic is the triangle of you, your baby, and your own mother. As you develop the motherhood mindset, the story of your own upbringing becomes critical. You may notice yourself wondering about your mother or other maternal figures in your life, and examining their suitability or unsuitability as models for your new role as mother.

ENSURING YOUR BABY'S SURVIVAL

Absolutely daunting for most new mothers is the realization that they suddenly hold the ultimate responsibility for someone else's life. This is a rare and highly charged situation for anyone, especially for a first-time mother. You might have considered yourself to be a very responsible person, but this absolute accountability is of another magnitude entirely. Besides literally keeping your baby alive, you are responsible for helping him grow and thrive. The kind of confidence and assurance that is needed to do this develops slowly once you begin to see with your own eyes that your baby is flourishing. With that success comes a quiet and profound sense of validation that you have the ability to give your child what she needs; that indeed, you are a mother.

SEEKING AFFIRMATION

All mothers want validation for their new identity, and to that end you will probably find yourself developing a special support network of family and friends, whether they live in the community or stay in touch by phone. It is important that the network be made up of past or present caregivers with lots of experience, which usually means a close circle of other mothers. Such networks make it safe for you to explore your fears and to start identifying your parental instincts and functions. The need to search for such a network is part of the motherhood mindset.

LOVING AND BEING LOVED

To a great extent, the way you love your baby will eventually permit him or her to love and be loved as well. Even though you probably felt as though you were getting to know your baby during the months of pregnancy, the newborn is really a mystery to the new mother. At the same time, there is an overpowering tug toward this little stranger. A new mother learns to allow herself to be loved by the baby. Keeping in touch emotionally with the ever-evolving bonds of love and attachment are also a part of the motherhood mindset.

FINDING ALTERED SENSIBILITIES

As a new mother, your responses to the world at large change and you develop completely new sensibilities with regard to what you notice, hear, and smell. As one mother explained,

> Soon after I had my baby I noticed a new set of reactions in myself. It started with a newscast on television about a catastrophic storm where they showed a mother reaching toward a house where her baby was trapped. There were tears in my eyes before I even knew I had reacted, and a sick feeling in my stomach. After that, any story which included the death or sickness of a child was almost unbearable for me. I stopped watching the news, and for a long time had to protect myself from newspaper and magazine articles that talked about

children getting hurt. It was as if I suddenly identified with all the world's mothers.

Many mothers I've spoken with describe this same reaction, marveling at how situations they used to take in stride look completely different when viewed through the eyes of a mother.

ACCEPTING YOUR INTUITION

Again and again, when you have a baby, you will find yourself acting without thinking. You will draw on maternal instincts, developing intuitive ways of holding, touching, and making sounds that build the relationship between you and your baby. Before too long, you will come to accept that as part of your new mindset you have an unexpected reservoir of intuitive responses and behaviors that you never accessed before.

Before the baby came you may have strived to maintain tight and rational control of your life. Maybe your work demanded predictable responses, or kept you in a recognizable routine day after day. With a baby, however, much of your time will be spent in spontaneous activities, requiring that you reach blindly into your bag of intuitions and come up with a suitable reaction on the spot. Some women adapt easily to this way of life, but for others it's quite difficult to operate in a realm where the rules are always shifting, and where you are not sure of the game to begin with. Even if you experience some difficulties, though, spontaneous reactions will become part of your new identity.

BALANCING BABY AND CAREER

For every woman, the merging of a new child and the mother's career is complicated at best. In general, the balance starts on the side of the baby, but in most cases, the birth of the baby heralds a long and tricky series of compromises for both parents and child. The decisions forced upon each mother and the solutions she chooses not only determine how her time is carved up, but also add another layer to her identity as a mother.

FINDING A NEW PLACE IN SOCIETY

It may not occur to you until your first outing with the baby, but society assigns a public role to motherhood that comes with inherent expectations. You can resist the role or accept it with pleasure, but you can't fully escape it. You are no longer a free agent in the world, responsible ultimately to yourself. Your new tasks as a mother are irrevocable. No matter how you feel or what you are thinking, you've become a mother in the eyes of the world.

One woman remembered,

> I took my baby to a town where I had walked so many times as a single and then a married woman. Always I had been aware of my attractiveness as an individual woman. Suddenly, holding a baby, I was no longer that same woman. I could see in people's eyes that they knew I was a mother, and looked at me as a unit with my baby. What a shock.

FINDING A NEW ROLE IN THE FAMILY

Society's view of you is powerful, but your family's view of you and the new baby can be even more dramatic. With the birth of your child you assume a new role in your original family and a pivotal part in the succession of generations. You are suddenly a player in the vast unfolding of our earth's history. Families know this, but don't talk about it, and the feeling of responsibility comes as a shock to some mothers. How could you explain this to someone before they experience it? Once more your identity gets altered in others' eyes, and eventually in your own as well.

WRITING A NEW CALENDAR

The day of your baby's birth will become the founding event of your new personal calendar, marking the start of an era. In years to come if someone asks you when you last traveled to California to see your brother, you'll say, "Let me see, the baby was just walking. I can remember him standing up in the airplane aisle, so it must have been four years ago. That would make it in 1996." You'll start reckoning time with two calendars, the one the rest of the world uses, and your private one, which follows your baby's age and developmental milestones.

DISCOVERING TASK OWNERSHIP

You've probably heard mothers talk about being on duty twenty-four hours a day, but never really thought about what it meant. The old expression "The buck stops here" takes on a new meaning for mothers. Twenty-four hours of every day you are the ultimate decision maker concerning your baby's life. There is no time off from being ultimately responsible, even if you delegate the actual work to someone else.

We call this sort of responsibility task ownership. You own the responsibility, so that any successes and failures, even if they are brought about by others, revert to you. Even if you share the tasks with your mate, as you will undoubtedly do, society has designated you the true task owner.

What this means in practical terms is that you will have to make split-second decisions even when you don't really know what to do and have never been there before. It's akin to being a CEO, a policeman on duty, or a physician on call. All eyes turn to the person in authority and expect that person to know what to do. When the baby cries in the middle of the night or breaks out in a rash or spits up its lunch, all eyes will turn to you.

On top of all the decisions you need to make while on unfamiliar terrain, it is also expected that you will automatically love your baby, make him or her grow, and successfully know how to teach him the basics of being a person. It is taken for granted that somehow you are qualified for the job even without any special training. One mother described this realization:

> On the way home from the hospital with my new baby, I sat in the backseat. I was staring at her when she suddenly began to cry in sharp little wails. There was no one to look to for help, no nurses, friends, or other mothers. I realized

with shock that I was the one. This was my baby, and I was supposed to know what to do with her. Though I tried to calm her, at the same time I felt a little wave of terror.

All these elements I've described contribute to the motherhood mindset. But beyond the changes to your inner landscape, as a new mother you will also have to deal with the peculiarities of our society and our time in history, both of which further impact your development as a mother.

MOTHERHOOD AND THE SOCIETY AT LARGE

In the last thirty years, one might have expected the feminist movement to lead the way in examining the inner world of the mother. It was the feminist movement that was the dominant force in recognizing reproductive rights and the rights of mothers in the workplace as issues central to combating the inequality of the sexes. However, for strategic reasons, the movement focused its attention where the need for equality was especially clear and compelling—the workplace, sports, politics—rather than the more problematic area of childbearing.

I have been startled not only by this silence, but by how rarely I find in exploring a mother's inner world, that the experience is described by mothers going through the process. My sense is that individual mothers know intuitively that every day they are experiencing powerfully new and all-consuming emotions—fierce love, aching protectiveness, a driving need to care for and nurture a new life—but scarcely know how to explain it to themselves, much less to another.

Neither have health professionals nor the society at large attended to this intimate psychological experience. As a society we easily talk about morning sickness, sore nipples, and new-mother fatigue. We publicly debate the benefits of nursing or bottle-feeding, and we thoroughly dissect a mother's dilemma of if and when to return to work. Politically we fight for better health care and family-leave policies, but we are strangely mute about the dramatic and often overwhelming changes going on in a mother's inner life.

Yet isn't it in this inner realm where mothers really live—facing unfamiliar waves of anxiety, desire, and uncertainty that accompany each day with a new baby? I have found in general that mothers don't know how much of their experience is common to all, and therefore don't know how to begin to talk about it. New mothers often wonder whether others are going through a similar upheaval, and if they do find the companionship of another new mother, spend most of their time together comparing and trying to put their feelings into words.

One of the main purposes of this book is to help you prepare for the dramatic changes you will encounter within yourself. Understanding some of the mental tasks and responsibilities that accompany almost all motherhood experiences can help you feel less stranded and uncertain when you feel them happening in your own life. The inner experiences of motherhood appear to be universal. In my own research, I have charted similarities in experience from multiple cultures, age groups, and social realms.

At this point you may ask how a man can write about

the inner world of a mother. Obviously, my being a man excludes me from ever personally experiencing the changes that come about in a woman's life as she prepares for and experiences childbirth. It doesn't, however, exclude me as a clinician from being able to observe and quantify those experiences over almost four decades of watching and interviewing new mothers.

To help me describe the material, I have collaborated with two women, both mothers and professionals. Nadia Bruschweiler-Stern, my wife, is a pediatrician and child psychiatrist, and Alison Freeland is a journalist with a long interest in parenting.

Both my wife and I have worked as therapists for women who were pregnant and entering the world of motherhood, and also have worked extensively with mothers having trouble in their parent-infant relationships. Nadia practices medicine in a pediatric setting caring for well babies as well as critically ill or handicapped children. I have interviewed and observed hundreds of mothers who volunteered to be subjects in various studies covering a baby's earliest ability to see, hear, remember, and respond emotionally to a situation and in even more studies specifically dealing with how mothers and babies interact in the daily activities of feeding and playing.

WHEN DOES A WOMAN BECOME A MOTHER?

In the course of discovering that mothers everywhere share a unique mindset, I also began to ask women at what point they felt they had really become mothers. I assumed the answer would be "When I gave birth, of course."

In fact, I learned by their responses that most mothers "become mothers" over and over again with mounting certainty, over a series of months. Their new identity may start at some point during the pregnancy, emerge more fully after the baby's birth, and then emerge full force after several more months of caring for the baby at home, when the woman realizes that she knows herself to be a mother in her own eyes. Each step of this realization is valid, yet with each step something is added to the motherhood identity.

In this way, the process of giving birth to the motherhood mindset progresses through phases. The new identity requires that you first prepare yourself mentally for the change, that you then undergo much emotional labor in bringing forth the new aspects of yourself, and finally that you work hard to integrate the changes into the rest of your life. All of this happens while you are nurturing a baby who demolishes your daily routines, keeps you up at night, and requires all of your attention. And yet, when you look back on your life, becoming a mother will remain one of your life's major endeavors.

BECOMING A MOTHER—A THREE-PART PROCESS

I have organized this book into three parts, corresponding to the three phases of becoming a mother.

Part 1, "Preparing to be a Mother," starts with the nine months of pregnancy, during which a woman performs most of the mental work required to prepare her for new motherhood. While her body forms the fetus, her mind actively prepares the way for her new identity.

You might think as I did that the actual birth of your baby will make you a mother. It appears, on the contrary, that the actual birth experience is still part of the preparation phase, and may give rise to a physical mother but not a psychological one. In Chapter 1 I talk about the pregnancy as a preparation and testing ground. During these nine months, a woman's imagination is fully engaged in hopes, dreams, fears, and fantasies about who her baby will be, what she will be like as a mother, and how her husband will be as a father. All these areas are still unknown, so a woman is free to project all kinds of ideas onto the stage of her mind about what life will be like when the baby arrives. This is vital preparation for becoming a mother.

Chapter 2 is about the role of the physical birth of the baby in moving the mother toward the psychological birth of her own motherhood. Chapter 3 deals with fantasies after the birth as they start to come into focus on a real baby, and how they often act as self-fulfilling prophecies. All together these three chapters describe the preparation phase.

Part 2, "A Mother Is Born," is about the months following the baby's birth. Only after a mother has returned home and engaged in the tasks of feeding, nurturing, and caring for the new baby does her motherhood mindset fully take form. Chapter 4 deals with the first task of motherhood, ensuring the survival of your baby, and the fears and questions that arise because of this most basic responsibility.

Chapter 5 covers the second hurdle you face as a new mother, that of forging an intimate relationship with your baby. This brings into play your whole personal history of relationships and how you experience intimacy. Fundamental questions may flicker across your mind: Will I love this baby? Will he or she love me? Will I be able to tell if our relationship is a good one? Will I be able to read my baby's signals and know how to respond to what she needs? How do I love this little being?

Chapter 6 brings up the third basic step of motherhood: your need for validation and encouragement from other mothers. This may include confronting your relationship with your own mother and deciding how much of it you want to repeat or reject in forming a relationship with your own child. You'll probably find yourself asking: Will I be like my own mother, and what does that mean?

Chapter 7 is one mother's personal account of how she struggled with these basic tasks of motherhood giving rise to her new identity. Gail and her son, Nikolai, illustrate how your own personal history influences the way you live out the first challenges of being a mother.

Chapter 8 is an extension of a book I wrote called *The Diary of a Baby*. In that book I was able to draw on years of clinical studies about what infants know and when they first know it. In the diary I tried to describe from the baby's point of view the various experiences of his world: his mother's love, feeding, light, movement, playing, and so on. In this chapter I show how an incident unfolds second by second from the baby's point of view, and at the same time interweave the mother's experience with the baby's to show how the two of them interact.

After you emerge from your first encounter with nurturing and caring for a baby, you will have effectively given birth to your new motherhood identity. For many months, however, while you tend to your newborn, this identity will be somewhat protected from the outside world. Part 3, "A

Mother Adapts," describes the integration of your new identity into the rest of your life.

Chapter 9 considers the challenges mothers of premature or handicapped babies face. These women have unique problems not only in forming their motherhood mindset but also in integrating it with the rest of their lives. They encounter many of the same situations as all mothers, only exaggerated in intensity or duration.

Chapter 10 takes up the inevitable question of if and when to resume your career after the birth of your baby. How does the motherhood identity mesh with that of a career woman?

Finally, in Chapter 11 fathers come to the foreground. A fatherhood realm exists in much the same way that a motherhood realm exists. A crucial aspect of this world is the fairly recent development of egalitarian households, where parents desire to share equally the tasks and responsibilities of the new baby. This chapter describes some of the adaptations necessary in a man's evolution from husband to father.

THE PATH TO THIS BOOK

The path to this book emerged after all my years of study, and after I wrote several books targeted toward members of my own profession. In 1977, I wrote a book called *The First Relationship: Infant and Mother*, about the minute behaviors, what I called the musical notes, that make up the symphony of the mother-infant relationship. In it I endeavored to describe the intricate choreography between mother and baby during playtime, putting to bed, and feeding.

I did the research for that book at a time when TV cameras had just become affordable tools of observation; I was able to watch a videotape of a mother and child over and over again, slowed down, speeded up, and freeze-framed. It was like being given a microscope suddenly making it possible to watch the tiniest interactions between a mother and child unfold.

Out of this work, our whole profession gained an immense appreciation of how much babies know and how socially competent they are in the first few months of life. Equally impressive were the complex intuitive behaviors of the mothers, most of which they performed without thinking. I geared this book for other researchers observing babies, and for mothers as well, but its main audience was my colleagues.

Armed with a fuller picture of an infant's ability to interact with its mother, and knowing what a mother could do instinctively to keep that interaction going, I tried to imagine how a baby views the world it shares with its parents. I realized that this new knowledge we were gathering was forcing us to change some of our clinical theories and practices. This resulted in a second book, *The Interpersonal World of the Infant*, published in 1985, also written for a clinical audience.

The next step for me was to focus even more on the inner world of the baby's experience. Clearly, babies can't tell you what's on—or in—their minds, but I still attempted to describe the world they live in by studying the vast body of information available about babies. In the past several decades there has been an explosion of research and understanding about the first few years of life: what babies see, hear, feel, and possibly think, and what they actually can learn and do. It is said now that we know more about the first year of life than about any of the later years.

Leaning heavily on this broad base of knowledge, I fashioned an imaginary baby, Joey, and constructed his likely thoughts, feelings, and perceptions about the ordinary events in his life. Making huge imaginative leaps from a solid base of scientific information, I wrote *The Diary of a Baby* mainly for parents, to give them a glimpse into their baby's world.

With ever-growing clinical experience, I grew naturally more interested in mothers and their personal histories. I was most struck by how a mother's private hopes, fears, and fantasies affected her relationship with her new baby. It became apparent that a mother's experiences within her family of origin played a decisive role in shaping how she would subsequently act with her own child. These observations led me to write *The Motherhood Constellation: A Unified View of Parent-Infant Psychotherapies*, again written to an audience of my fellow clinicians.

It was my work on this last book that led me into further exploration of the inner world of the mother. This task was easier than exploring the baby's inner world because I can hear a mother talk about her inner experiences, whereas I could only guess at a baby's inner experience by observation.

The more my colleagues and I listened to what mothers were saying, the more convinced we became that the mother's inner world is what guides her interactions with her child, be it feeding, playing with, or caring for her baby. We are beginning to understand that the mother-child relationship as well as the future development of the child depend in large part on what's going on in the mother's mind and is based on her personal history.

This book represents the completion of a journey. I started with exploring the interactions of a mother and her baby, then went more fully into the baby's life, and am now delving deeper into the mother's inner world. *The Birth of a Mother,* describing the new mother's inner world, becomes the companion book to *The Diary of a Baby* with its description of the baby's inner life. Together they form a whole picture of two inner worlds converging on the same events.

Over the past few years, as both Nadia and I have studied further and as I lecture around the world on these topics, I hear the same responses over and over again. One common response is "Well, Dr. Stern, I think the things you have to say about the motherhood mindset are obvious once I hear them. But it seems my grandmother could have told me the same thing."

My point is that your grandmother could have told you these things, but didn't. Neither did your obstetrician, or your older sister, or your own mother. The motherhood mindset may be obvious, but in our society, it is rarely discussed.

Another often heard response from mothers is "You have described my experience exactly, but I didn't know what it was until I heard it. I've never been able to put it into words."

And yet another response comes from women working in the mental health professions who were trained to believe, as I was, that mothers do not make up a unique population. These mental health professionals face the same conflicting information that led me to write this book. Often I hear them say, "As a woman and a mother, I know what you're describing is true, but it contradicts my clinical background. What are you suggesting we do, follow what we believe instinctively or stick with what we have been taught theoretically? At this point I don't know whether to thank you or curse you for this information."

Indeed, we do hope that this book will have the further value of altering some current therapeutic practices concerning parent and infant mental health.

Our central task, then, is to present a picture of the motherhood mindset, to shed light on this inner realm and bring it out of hiding by describing it and giving it its own language. By doing so I hope to help mothers validate their own experiences and discover words for what they've already sensed intuitively. In addition, perhaps this book can take the edge off the loneliness and isolation so many mothers experience when they face the dramatic change in their inner landscape, and don't know whether they are the only ones to whom it's ever happened.

Another aim of the book is to help mothers practice their craft of motherhood. It is certainly a craft that is learned by experience and apprenticeship, not by formal teaching. The real transmission of the craft occurs during walks in the park with other mothers, standing in line with a woman in a similar situation, or being able to remember what one's own mother or grandmother did.

Working from the voices of so many mothers makes this book a kind of apprentice handbook, revealing what it is like to live the experience, and what sort of transformation is likely to take place in your life when you have a baby.

In another way, this is also a book of prevention.

Ordinary life with a baby is made up of recurring hourly interactions as you put your baby to sleep (or try to), feed her, change her, play with her, regulate her activity level, set limits for her, and teach her about the world. Of the thousands of hourly tasks involving your baby, the majority of them will not run smoothly, nor take place in a way you can predict. In fact, struggling with these interactions is a large part of what motherhood is about in the first years. These are also the very activities that easily become problem points for both the baby and the parent.

It is in these activities that the mother's hopes, fears, and fantasies, as well as her own childhood memories, start to play out, and actually influence the development of the new baby. Becoming familiar with one's own inner life and how it may affect the baby helps a new mother recognize when she is facing a problem point and, further, helps her find a solution that is appropriate to her situation.

Ultimately, better understanding the motherhood mindset and the phases of its development demystifies some of this new world you have entered, gives you greater confidence, and enables you to draw deeper pleasure from the new identity you have given birth to psychologically.

PART I

Preparing to Be a Mother

ONE

Pregnancy: Preparation for Your New Identity

I T IS FAIRLY well documented that by the age of two and a half children have established their gender identity. This means that from your earliest years as a little girl you begin to form ideas and snatches of fantasies about yourself as a possible mother in the future. These vague notions of what it means to be a mother grow more detailed later in childhood, and even more so during adolescence. They take on new meanings entirely when you fall in love and choose a partner. The process goes into high gear when you discover you're pregnant and begin to prepare for motherhood in earnest.

During pregnancy, as your body undertakes the physical formation of a fetus, your mind undertakes the formation of an idea of the mother you might become. At the same time, you start to construct a mental picture of what you think your baby will be like. In a sense, there are three pregnancies going on simultaneously: the physical fetus growing in your womb, the motherhood mindset developing in your psyche, and the imagined baby taking shape in your mind.

At this time you are invariably preoccupied with wishes, fears, and fantasies that, in our culture, revolve around several straightforward questions. Who is this baby? How will I be as a mother? How will my perceptions about myself and the life I've been leading change? What will happen to my marriage? My career? My relationships with my family and friends? And most persistent, How will the delivery be? And will my baby be born healthy? These preoccupations provide the raw material you work with in preparing your motherhood identity.

People rarely think about such issues in a systematic way, but rather grapple with them on and off during the many days of pregnancy. For some it is a gradual process. For others, there are dramatic moments of reappraisal and redefinition. Often the issues get worked on subliminally, weaving in and out of your daydreams, night dreams, nightmares, or inchoate feelings. Your imagination works at full capacity to try to give form to the life you will be leading, which at this time you can scarcely comprehend.

You play out imagined scenarios with imagined characters—imagined baby, the imagined self-as-mother, the imagined father-to-be, the imagined grandparents. Each of these is created, undone, and put together again from a different starting point, many times over. The mind during pregnancy is a workspace where the future is assembled and worked over like an invention in progress.

I can best explain this imagining process by telling a story about nurses and real newborns. The child psychiatrist Stephen Bennett listened in as the nurses in a newborn section of a hospital went about their daily tasks, and spent so much time around them that they began to talk as if he weren't there. His study reveals how anyone who is continually in the presence of a baby (as a mother is with the baby inside her or as a newborn) projects personality traits onto that baby. Adults quickly dip into a repertoire of personality traits from their life experience, and choose ones to attribute to the baby.

Each nurse followed this pattern. For instance, she would call one little girl The Princess. This baby was always petite with delicate features and an easy disposition. Another baby she would call Killer. This one was always an active, alert boy with a contagious smile who would presumably one day knock women dead with his charm and good looks. In the same small nursery there might also be a Terror, Her Royal Highness and a Professor.

The nurses made these attributions of character type very quickly. After all, the babies only stayed in the nursery a few days. The cast of characters depended upon the particular nurse and the physical and temperamental features of each infant. Of course, each nurse had a somewhat different assortment of nicknames that she assigned. There were a few cultural favorites, however, so there was almost always a Princess and a Killer, even if these titles were passed on to new babies every few days as the nursery population turned over.

In the same way, you as a mother-to-be will make guesses about your baby, before and after he is born. These guesses are guided by your hopes and fears and your own past history, and they reveal much about your priorities and values. The fantasies you have about who your baby will grow up to be are quite revealing about what you care about. Every mother mentally constructs the baby of her hopes and dreams and also of her fears. Mothers also extend their imaginations to include what the baby will be like at one year, as a schoolgirl, and as an adult. Often a mother will create a contradictory and even amusing patchwork of traits for her child. One woman told me that her musings would have made her son an unlikely combination of Albert Einstein and Mel Gibson. And why not? She is exploring the traits that are important to her, and saying that she wants a son who is brilliant as well as sexy.

Some mothers insist they do not make up imagined babies, but even in choosing a name, they betray their desire for a certain kind of child. A name can indicate loyalty to a family and ethnic background, or the desire to break away from that same background. It indicates what type of person you admire and secretly hope your baby will be.

For a long time psychologists and psychiatrists believed that these imaginary babies were rare, and when present, indicated that the mother had problems. But after much more clinical experience we have come to see that this imagining process goes on constantly in all mothers. It seems to be a helpful and creative way to prepare for the situations you will soon find yourself in—not just mental wool gathering.

Most of us, not just mothers-to-be, create imaginary worlds on and off during our everyday lives. Such an imaginary world is like a mental stage where we can invent and play out different possible outcomes and solutions to the situations we find ourselves in. They help us survive. As you become more aware of your motherhood role and responsibilities, these scenarios will help you and your baby survive too. The story of your imagined baby and your whole entrance into the realm of motherhood are inextricably entwined.

From interviewing many mothers and mothers-to-be, we have come to recognize some common patterns in these imaginings. The most common pattern is that until a woman is certain of the viability of her pregnancy (generally during the twelfth week), she doesn't let herself think too specifically about the baby she will have. This is especially true if she has lost a fetus before or considers her pregnancy to be at risk for any reason. (If you have experienced a miscarriage, you already know that a large part of the grief comes from the loss of what you imagined and hoped for.)

I knew a mother of two boys who was devastated when she had a miscarriage because she felt sure that she was finally going to have a girl. She went on to have two more boys, but for all her life longed for that imagined daughter she had lost, although she never really knew if the lost fetus was a girl or not.

In general, after the third month, once the doctor gives the green light regarding the viability of the pregnancy, the imagining process really takes off. At this point most new mothers start to play with more and more specific personality and physical traits that their baby could exhibit. Some women, however, need more than three months to assimilate the fact that they are pregnant. Even at the end of the first trimester, they aren't yet ready to engage their imaginations, and even may avoid telling others that they are pregnant.

Diana, about whom you'll read more in these pages, waited until almost the fifth month before publicly announcing her pregnancy. She instinctively wanted to protect herself from others' expectations of what she was supposed to think and feel, and when. She needed to follow her own timetable and was tuned in to its pace.

Emily announced her pregnancy as soon as the home test registered positive, in her second week. She could hardly wait for the world to know. But Emily's concerns in life were different from Diana's. She wanted desperately to integrate her pregnancy and the baby-to-come into her larger family, and immediately began mentally to elaborate on her imagined child and on what her life as a mother would be like. Most women, striking a balance between excitement about the pregnancy and fear of loss, announce their pregnancy at the third month.

During the fourth month, experience with your real fetus gives your imagined baby a large push forward. This comes about in one of two ways. Sonograms of the fetus are almost routine these days. The visual image of the real fetus—the curve of the vertebral column that looks like a pearl necklace, the sound of the heartbeat, the sight of the baby moving—is breathtaking. Many expectant couples today carry around wallet-sized sonograms much as they will baby pictures later on.

Even without a sonogram, you can feel the fetus begin to kick at about four months, providing irrefutable evidence of the baby to come. Mothers often picture the baby's motions in utero, and add them to their growing profile of the imagined baby. A mother might say, "This baby is a really decisive kicker. He's going to be the kind of person who can't wait to get on with life." Or, "This baby always kicks when she hears music. I know she'll be musical." Or, "It's as if this baby kicks in accordance with my moods, like he's already tuned in to me." The imagined baby is, of course, purely subjective, so the same kick could inspire the mother to imagine any of these possible character traits.

Between the fourth and seventh months is when most mothers-to-be usually give the freest rein to their imaginations, and all the while, the baby in the mind's eye becomes more elaborately drawn. By the seventh or eighth month, the imagined baby is probably as fully constructed as he will be during the pregnancy.

Then, during the eighth and ninth months, something very interesting happens. Instead of the imagined baby becoming even more fully drawn, almost the opposite occurs. Recent studies suggest that at this time, the mother starts to undo this highly elaborated imagined baby. She allows the mental picture to fade, and in a sense starts to dismantle and even hide the imagined baby from herself.

One has to ask why, though upon further consideration, this shift makes profound sense. At birth, the real baby and the imagined one will meet for the first time, and the mother cannot afford to have too great a difference between the two. She must protect the real baby and herself from large discrepancies between the expectations she created in her mind—be they those of sex, size, looks, coloring, or temperament—and her real baby. She must clear the decks so that she and the real baby can start to work together without interference from past baggage.

The imagined baby doesn't completely disappear, however. Usually some last-minute adjustments are made just before the real birth. In the first two trimesters of your pregnancy, you probably based your imagined baby's traits (especially the positive ones) on your husband or father, if you think you'll be having a boy, or on your mother if you're having a girl. As you progress toward term, you start to discard the idea of others' traits, and begin to see yourself as the major contributor to your baby's character and life. As the birth approaches, you start to claim this baby more strongly as your own.

During her fifth month of pregnancy, Margaret envisioned that her baby-to-be would have the forceful character of her mother and the social ease of her husband. Three months later, when she speculated about her baby, she decided she still wanted the baby to have a forceful character, but maybe to be more flexible and adaptable, like herself. And although she hoped the baby could be socially adept, she really hoped he or she would be restrained and private, like her.

So as the birth draws near, you will find yourself claiming more of the territory. This may be a necessary step toward establishing your own primary relationship with your baby when he or she arrives. Moving everyone else to the wings puts you and the real baby at center stage. As the main characters in the first act of this new drama, you and your baby need to be the focus of attention. The proprietary impulse to bring the baby up in your image, no one else's, is a fierce feeling for new mothers, and in fact some women at this point in their pregnancies have trouble including even their husbands in their exclusive imaginary circle.

Now, suppose that a woman gives birth prematurely, at seven or eight months of gestation. The mother will not have had enough time to undo her imagined baby. She and the real baby now suffer doubly. Not only is the real baby less developed than normally expected, but the mother compares it to her often unrealistically idealized, imaginary baby who is still too vivid in her mind. The woman's motherhood mindset is premature and psychologically fragile at this point.

The mother of a preemie is particularly vulnerable for other reasons as well. She often feels like an incomplete person who could not properly finish her pregnancy, even if the circumstances were totally beyond her control. Furthermore, she is physically separated from her baby, who often stays in an intensive-care unit, leaving her feeling impotent to attach to the baby who is not next to her. She has to watch others do the caregiving, in most cases hospital staff who are more expert than she could possibly be. She is in a strange environment where she feels anything but at home, and she may also suffer from the effects of a hormonal disequilibrium. Finally, her expectations for the imagined baby are at their highest while the reality of the real, premature baby is at its least advantageous.

There is yet one more reason for her vulnerability. In the last few months before term, fears of the delivery and for the baby's health occupy a large and important place in most women's minds, and frequently contribute to the arrest of any further elaboration of the image of the imagined baby. There is a wide array of normal fears, many of which visit almost all mothers-to-be. There are the common fears of the baby being born dead, or dying at birth, of the mother not being able to bear the pain, or of being so small that the baby will get stuck and be unable to come out. A mother may have heard that the umbilical cord can wrap around the baby's neck, or she may picture herself giving birth in a place where no one can help. There are fears of a breech baby, of a deformed baby or even a monster. In the last months of pregnancy many mothers report vivid, frightening dreams such as giving birth to kittens, or of babies whirling around in spirals. All these thoughts are quite common and seem to be part of the process.

In most pregnancies, it is important to grapple with these thoughts for a while if they are not too intense or persistent. While contemplating these scenarios in advance could never fully prepare a woman for the worst, it may act as part of the preparation for all eventualities of the motherhood realm. The mother of a preemie doesn't have time to pass through this phase entirely.

Here is what one mother of a preemie described to me:

The first time I saw her was so strange I didn't know what to feel. Part of me wanted to run away. Part of me felt like I was outside of my life watching it happen to someone else. She wasn't supposed to be here yet, or to be so little. I could hardly find her in the middle of all the medical paraphernalia, lying in her glass box with her eyes closed and her tiny chest heaving up and down like a bird's. She was tiny and almost blue. Her arms and legs seemed as thin as the tubes going in and out of her body.

I wanted to hold her. I had dreamed of that and what it would feel like. But she looked so fragile I could have hurt her. I was afraid, even a little repulsed . . . it's horrible to say but true. My body was in turmoil, and nothing was ready. We should have still been at home waiting for her to arrive in another eight weeks.

I was going to take the last month to fix up her room—it's all planned in my head—and to organize her clothes. But I don't even have anything small enough for her to wear, even the beautiful dress that was my grandmother's. I think I was expecting a baby like my brother just had, pink and round, and substantial, even pretty. Gina (that's the name I always had for this baby) was going to be robust and magnificent. In that weird place, I didn't know where to stand, or what to do, or what the nurses wanted of me. The nurses were more comfortable with Gina than I was, and I am her mother.

Nothing was ready. Her room wasn't, she wasn't, and God knows I wasn't.

This mother was caught between her real baby and her imagined baby. Her preparatory work for entering into the realm of motherhood had been cut short. Under normal circumstances a woman has the eighth and ninth months to get herself ready to meet her real baby.

ATTACHMENT

An immense area of study concerning new motherhood is the attachment that develops between mother and baby. How you form the bonds of intimacy with your child is a matter of great importance, and depends in large part upon your personal history and experience. Although each mother attaches to her child in a unique way, most women follow one of three general patterns; and as is the case with so many aspects of motherhood, this occurs for the most part unconsciously.

Not surprisingly, the attachment process begins during pregnancy with a woman's thoughts and imaginings about her unborn child. Let's look at the three common attachment patterns and hear the thoughts of three different women during their pregnancies. The way these women imagine their babies will affect their marriages, their lifestyles, and their own souls.

The first pattern is followed by women who tend to keep the motherhood experience at a distance in order to deal with it. First of all, they appear to be less totally absorbed by their pregnancies than might be expected, though that may not be true on the inside. When they think about their original families, they tend to take a long step or two back, and be dismissive of their own history, including details about how they were mothered. They act as if their history with their parents isn't particularly relevant to what is happening now. They may or may not be very emotionally involved with the process of becoming a mother, but in any event they will not let themselves fully face the issue, and certainly will not talk with you about it.

These women exhibit what clinicians call the *dismissing attachment pattern*. They can see the entire panorama of their family relations, but the view is from a safe distance. Diana exemplifies this style. Diana was the woman mentioned previously who waited five months before telling others she was pregnant and probably didn't fully believe it herself until then.

A very different attachment pattern is followed by women who become so involved in the motherhood experience that they don't take any steps back to get some perspective on the process. They conform to the *enmeshed attachment pattern.* This applies particularly to their reflections on their own mothers, with whom they remain very close during their pregnancies and beyond. They remain as enmeshed in their relationship with their mothers as they will most likely be in their relationship with their babies to come. In general, women in this enmeshed attachment pattern tend to throw themselves into their primary relationships without reflecting on them. Emily, who told her family immediately when she became pregnant, exemplifies this category.

The third type of mother occupies a place between the other two. She is willing to lose herself in her relationship with her infant, and also become involved with her mother in the present, but in a measured fashion. Her past experiences as a little girl with her mother evoke many thoughts and feelings in her, but she can also take a large step back to reflect on her experiences as both a mother and a daughter. These women who view their lives from the middle distance are said to exhibit an *autonomous attachment pattern.* Margaret is an example of this type.

Although no one woman completely exemplifies one pattern, most tend to fit into one of these three groups. All three styles are normal, representing different ways of adapting to the psychological turbulence that becoming a mother entails.

To show the pervasive nature of the mental planning, preparing, testing, and rehearsing that takes place during pregnancy, I have chosen to take a snapshot of what each of these three mothers mused about when they were six months pregnant.

These reflections offer a glimpse into how three different women think and feel about their changing world. Each immerses herself quite differently in her pregnancy experience, and each has a different style of reflecting upon and talking about herself in her new role as a pregnant woman. Each is also celebrating a birthday, which provides a natural point for them to pause and examine the course of their lives.

Diana, the view from far away

Driving down Ridge Street, I have to decide my next move. Either I stop at the grocery store or drive straight home. This is a typical conflict for me, and harder in some ways than any of the decisions I make at work. It's my birthday, and Carl will be at home preparing a special dinner for me. He knows better than to surprise me, so I already know about the dinner and what he's cooking. I hope he doesn't get inventive and decide to invite a few friends. I don't feel like entertaining right now.

My grocery store problem arises because I'm sure we're going to have good coffee with dessert, and I'm equally sure Carl has forgotten to buy half-and-half. Since I've been pregnant I've virtually given up all of life's pleasures—coffee, wine, candy, and potato chips. Tonight I'm going to splurge on the coffee, but it won't be as good without the cream. However, if I buy the cream, Carl will know that I think he's forgotten it, and will probably be insulted. I pull into the parking lot anyway. I really want that cream.

Another uncomfortable moment takes place when I get out of the car. At six months pregnant, I can no longer cover my bulging waist. I've always prided myself on presenting a fairly nice figure, and have grown used to at least several glances when I walk down the street. Forget those glances now. I'm getting bigger all the time, and am actually a little irritated at losing control over my body shape. It's for a good cause, I tell myself, that I've turned into a lumpy, out-of-proportioned woman. One thing I will not do is waddle. I refuse to waddle.

I wonder if I'll ever get my figure back. At thirty-seven it's a sobering thought. Carl and I didn't decide not to have children all these years, we just never let it happen. But lately it seemed as if I was approaching the point of no return. It was now or never.

In the office today, my associates gave a nod of acknowledgment to my birthday, but our receptionist, Donna, actually gave me a gift. There was a tissue paper present on my desk, and inside was a little white cap with pink ribbon ties. It's as sweet as it can be, and is probably in the bag right now under the seat. I think Donna's more excited about this baby than I am.

While I make my way toward the dairy department, I think about my mother's phone call today. She said she sent me money for my birthday. No surprises there. It's in the mail, and I should put it toward the baby. She didn't have a clue what to get, so now the burden is on me. I suppose Mother will come after we have the baby, but I don't expect she'll be a lot of help. When I picture someone helping, I picture Donna. It's funny. I never thought much about Donna until now, but she suddenly seems like someone who understands babies. Maybe I was born without the gene that understands. I'm not sure I'm going to be very good at this.

Carl, on the other hand, is going to be a great father. He's so easygoing. Truthfully, he has to be to put up with me. I know I'm not exactly easy. Even my doctor told me to lighten up. I took the amnio test and they said everything will be fine. But I figure they can't test for everything. For instance, no one can predict if this is going to be what they call an easy baby, or a hard one. She's going to have to be easy, like Carl. He jokes about being a low-maintenance husband, which is a good thing, considering my abilities in the cooking and cleaning category. She'll be low maintenance, too, if she knows what's good for her. I don't think I'm sounding very maternal right now.

I've made it through the grocery store, cream in hand, and I'm headed home. I'm thirty-seven years old, lumpy, and I want my coffee with cream. This poor baby. What if she's like me? Let's hope not. And let's hope she's a real sleeper. Right now I'm most concerned about getting the right kind of help for this event. Donna says there's no sleep for new parents. Well, I don't know how I can live with that. I'm a real bear when I'm tired. If this kid stays up at night? Well, we'll see.

Diana can't think very long without coming around to the subject of her baby-to-be. Although she is quite preoccupied with her pregnancy, Diana holds herself farther away from the event, and takes such a long view as to sound almost unfeeling about it, as well as about her own mother. Truly Diana sounds a lot tougher than she is, and in reality is dealing with all of the same subjects as Emily and Margaret do, only from a more distant standpoint.

Emily, the close-up view

I knew my family would do something for my birthday this year, but I didn't expect them to all show up at the house. Poor David. He gets thrown out of his own kitchen whenever Mom is around. She takes over when it comes to food.

I love coming home from work lately and putting on this big soft sweatshirt. You can really see my belly now, and sometimes I slide down on the couch and let it stick up in the air. Now that I'm six months along, everyone knows it's a baby and I'm not just fat. Finally!

At work I don't think about it too much except when my sisters or my mom call. I guess I do get too many personal calls these days, but after all. . . My sister Barbara thinks she has to tell me everything, just because she's already had a baby. But she moved away, and I'm glad we live near my parents.

David's family is a different story. They're so into their old culture; it's almost like they don't even know they're in America. But I don't know what I'd do without my parents around. We see them so much, and now that the baby's coming, they're overjoyed.

Everyone thought we'd wait a while to get pregnant. Even I thought we'd wait at least three years, long enough for David to get on his feet with the business. Now we don't totally need my salary. I suppose we sort of accidentally-on-purpose got pregnant. The business is doing fine, and I don't want to be too old when we have kids. Twenty-five isn't too old. This is my last birthday without a baby.

My birthday gifts this year are pretty funny. You'd think it was a baby shower and not a birthday. Of course Barbara sends something totally practical—a breast pump. I don't think I'll use it much. It looks like it might hurt. Mom and Dad give me the nicest stuff. Sometimes I feel guilty that David and I rely on them so much. For my birthday Mom is going to take me stroller shopping.

It's great we're having a girl. Barbara's baby is a boy, but she doesn't live close enough for us all to see him very often. I think Mom wanted a granddaughter. She certainly knows how to raise girls, and she's going to be able to help me a lot. There wasn't a question about what we would name this baby. When I found out it was a girl, I knew she'd be Carrie, after my grandmother. I hope she gets my grandmother's legs, and her singing voice, too. Mom would love that. Those characteristics seem to have skipped over the rest of us.

Dad and David have escaped to the porch to talk about the business and let the rest of us talk about babies. I'm amazed I'm so into this whole thing. Today on my lunch hour I bought a pair of tiny sneakers. There's nothing cuter than baby clothes. It's crazy, but this baby's closet is almost full already. I know Mom is knitting things. She's so prepared, she's probably already made meals and frozen them for when I go into the hospital.

Dinner is the usual circus tonight. Everyone takes a plate and heaps it full of Mom's lasagna. It's my favorite, so everyone gets to eat it on my birthday. Only one dark cloud passes over all night. For some reason my little sister mentions cousin Anne, and I wish she hadn't. Anne had a baby last year. The birth was really hard, and the baby still isn't right. They think it might be cerebral palsy. I don't even want to hear about that right now. It makes me crazy. My sister shouldn't have said anything. Not while I'm pregnant.

When the house finally empties, David and I can talk. When he saw the little sneakers I bought today, he thought I was nuts. Sometimes I think he thinks I'm going overboard with this whole pregnancy thing. He could be right, but I can't help it.

Emily is so close to the other members of her family, her mother in particular, that she almost can't see herself as separate from them. Diana, on the other hand, keeps her mother at a safe distance. Margaret seems to balance herself in the middle.

Margaret, the middle view

We walk into the dining room of my favorite restaurant, and as soon as I see the lights on the harbor outside, I relax. Being near the water always calms me and in this case helps me stop being mad at Jim.

We always come to this restaurant for special occasions, and tonight is really significant for me. I am thirty today. Too bad Jim forgot a file in his office and made us late. And too bad he waited so long to invite my parents to join us. Now they have another commitment and can't come. Jim is probably glad they're not here, but I'd like to see them. Enough of this. I want to enjoy myself.

Taking off my coat, I realize why the evening is especially significant. I finally look pregnant. Six months, and my blouse drapes neatly over my round belly. Now everyone can see what shape I'm in. Men are funny. When an attractive woman comes into a room, men notice. They look up, take in the view, and look back to their partner. It's almost pure reflex. I've never put this into words before because it's not the kind of thing you can really prove. When I take off my coat tonight, the glances are different. Some men hardly look. Others take me in with their eyes and give me a genuine smile. It's not sexy or furtive, just appreciative. I guess maybe they're fathers.

Lately I've connected with women differently, too. Mothers look at me with excitement and knowingness. I don't have a clue what I'm in for with this baby, but whatever it is, it's dramatic enough to connect me with complete strangers.

"Table for two?" the waiter asks. "And soon it will be table for three, I see." People certainly feel free to comment on my pregnancy now that it's clear. It's such a public condition. Jim leaves me at the table alone for a minute, and I stare at the lights on the water. The waiter is right, soon it will be a table for three. I think I'll probably miss not having time alone with Jim anymore, but maybe I'll automatically love this baby so much that it won't matter. Don't mothers automatically love their babies?

I know I'm already attached to this baby inside me. At work I rub my stomach under the drafting table and feel a kind of secret joy. I think I'll be an okay mom. Jim will be a good dad too. I'm going to make sure he gets up at night to help with feeding. I'm not doing this whole thing by myself.

In the reflection in the window I can see Jim returning to the table. I thought he might do something a little special tonight, but it doesn't look like it. He's even been a little distant, which isn't like him. But when he sits down across from me, he takes both my hands in his and looks right into me with his eyes, and I forgive whatever distance may have been there. He's good at intimacy. Sometimes I think he's more sensitive than I am. I wonder if our baby will be sensitive like Jim. I hope so. But I hope he's not too sensitive either. I don't want him to get hurt in life. Then again, the baby could be like my brother and never tune in to people at all. No, I think he'll be like Jim.

If the baby is a girl, it's okay if she's sensitive. But I think she'll be smart, too, and good at whatever she does, like my side of the family. What if she has Jim's looks and my personality? Then she could be a handsome architect. That reminds me of the office and the little party they gave me today. What a difference. Last year I had to buy the donuts for my own birthday. This year they got me a cake and gave me a mobile to hang over the baby's crib. They sang "Happy Birthday," and then looked at me as if I were never coming back or something. I said, "Hey, I'm not dying. I'm having a baby." I'm the first one of our group to get pregnant, and they think I'm going to change. I doubt I could change so much that I wouldn't come back to work.

One thought sort of nags me, though. My mother worked before she had me, but she never went back. She had a pretty good job in a law office, and could certainly have had a good career, but she stayed home with me instead. Of course, that was a different generation, and they didn't need the money, and then my brother came along nine years later, which really kept her at home. I still wonder. Did she think she would return to work, and then find out she didn't want to?

I've been looking at Mom differently these days. She was about my age when she had me, so I wonder if she was nervous and excited just like I am. It's hard to picture; she's so self-assured now. I can't imagine her waddling with a big belly. She's always been glad I became an architect, but she's really glad I'm pregnant. She even pulled out my old bassinet and mentioned she knew where she could have it spruced up and fitted with sheets. It's as if my work was fine, but now I'm getting down to what I really should be doing in life—having a baby.

I'm thinking so hard about my mother that it scarcely seems odd to see her reflection in the window. But she and my father are somewhere else tonight. Then I turn my head and see Jim with a little grin on his face, and then realize that not only my mother but also my father and brother are walking toward us across the dining room. "Surprise," they say in unison, and our waiter pulls an empty table next to ours so they can join us.

Slowly I figure out Jim really didn't forget a file in his office, or forget to call my parents. He had the whole thing planned after all. Why was I mad at him? When the waiter wheels a dessert cart over to us, another follows wheeling a stroller with a big bow on it. My parents planned that part.

As the evening winds down, I look around the table. Dad is telling a funny story to Jim, while Mom quietly pulls the stroller over and begins examining it. My brother seems most interested in the two girls eating behind me. This is my family, full of peculiarities. And Jim and I are about to start a family of our own. It makes me wonder what peculiarities our new little family will have.

If you had been listening in on Margaret's thoughts a year earlier, they would have been completely different. She most likely would have been preoccupied with her relationship with Jim and the ups and downs of her work life. Now, however, her pregnancy has become the new, central organizing theme of her existence. For the first time, she's starting to wonder what her mother was like at her age, and why she really didn't go back to work after having a baby. She's thinking about her mother, herself, and her baby all at once, and she's analyzing everyone's personality in light of how their traits might show up in her child. Margaret drifts between feelings and stepping back to examine her feelings with perspective. Without fully realizing it, Margaret now experiences all events in light of what her life will be like once she has a baby.

In these birthday musings we can see how each woman deals with the same issues, yet works on them very differently. Each has her own style, which determines in a large part how the issues are experienced. Emily views her growing body with excitement, while Diana wishes she could cover up the whole thing. Margaret allows herself to wonder how much she will be like her own mother, while Diana gives it very little thought. Emily doesn't consider what traits her husband might pass on to their baby, while Margaret identifies different parts of her husband's personality and "tries them on" her imagined baby.

Each woman has also developed a consciousness about her changing body. Whether you enjoy them or not, the physical changes in your body during pregnancy greatly assist your mental preparation for motherhood. For nine months you live with the constant reality of a changing body. Your breasts grow and have a different weight. Your belly swells, shifting your center of gravity so that you stand, walk, sit, and get up from a chair differently. The baby's movements plus your body's external changes are a constant reminder of the baby-to-be. In this way you live for almost nine months in an intimate relationship with your future baby as your body pushes thoughts about the baby upon you.

For all of us, our identities are deeply connected to the experience and image we have of our bodies. Think about the dramatic shifts in an adolescent's identity as his or her body starts to change. It is similar for a pregnant woman whose body alters about as much as an adolescent's, only far more rapidly. A pregnant woman has only seven months (the first two may not count) to assimilate these changes, while an adolescent may have a few years. Such rapid body changes destabilize a woman's body image, and prepare the ground for a new organization of her identity.

While the physical reality of pregnancy plays a huge role in preparing most women for motherhood, it is obviously not indispensable, since women who adopt babies develop the motherhood mindset without the aid of these bodily changes. But it may take more work for them to do so. Women who adopt still have a period of time during which their imagination constructs the baby of their dreams and they imagine themselves as mothers, and very often they have more than nine months, as the adoption process can stretch out for years.

Under most conditions, then, your changing body not only frees up your previous sense of self so that the motherhood identity can take hold, it also cultivates the development of an imagined baby. The nine months of pregnancy prepare you in an indispensable way for the motherhood to come. This time introduces many of the themes that will be relevant in forming your motherhood identity, but the process occurs in your imagination, where you can revise and rehearse many different future scenarios. By the time your pregnancy reaches term, the main portion of the mental preparation for your new identity is in place.

TWO

Giving Birth: A Time of Transition

IF YOU ASK people when a woman becomes a mother, the quick answer is "When she gives birth, of course." But it is not that simple. The actual moment of birth may be the moment when a woman physically becomes a mother, but the psychological birth of a mother takes longer and has many more phases than just labor and delivery. If you can get a mother to slow down her memories and really think about the day or night she gave birth for the first time, she will probably agree that as incredibly intense as the experience was, it did not in fact make her a mother right away. The birth itself is more a moment of transition when the woman hangs suspended in time—tired, elated, and relieved.

This chapter is not intended to describe in detail the entire process of giving birth, but only to signal some of the key events in the process that lead women toward their motherhood identity. At the moment of birth, the new mother is not yet attached to her baby. There is the tug of a deeply familiar being, but he is still a stranger. She does not yet realize what it is to care for her baby. Only when she does will her motherhood be pulled into being.

After many years of talking with women about their motherhood experiences, it is clear to me that almost without exception, the birth of her baby (especially the first one) is a central event in a woman's life, in equal parts miraculous and traumatic, packed with unforgettable emotions and implications. For most women, it is an event so primitive and profound as to be difficult to fully assimilate or put into words. It is a story that never gets fully told, not even to the mother herself, and therefore remains a partially known, unmovable cornerstone in the construction of her life story. Whether the birth experience was good, or bad, or a mix of the two doesn't matter. The memory remains vivid, no matter what.

The narration of your baby's birth will become an important part of your motherhood identity. My wife and I together have asked many women what it was like for them to give birth the first time. Almost without exception, they retell the story with a clarity that has the freshness of the original experience. It doesn't matter if the birth occurred four days, or four years, or four decades earlier, the memory has the same intensity. Interestingly, most women's stories undergo some changes with time and retelling. The tale becomes a combination of fact, fancy, and myth, but whatever its composition, it remains a guiding life narrative marking the road to motherhood.

When you look back on the birth of your first baby, there may be parts of the experience you wish had gone differently, or that still disturb you today. In some cases the birth experience and its small or big events may have influenced the early direction of the mother-baby relationship. It also may well have influenced your future feelings about doctors, nurses, and hospitals.

This dramatic event, the birth, is one of the final steps in the preparation for becoming a mother. Again, each woman experiences the key moments in the process differently, but for all, the birth goes a long way toward putting the motherhood identity into place. Obviously a woman can feel herself to be a mother even if she virtually misses the birth process, as in the case of adoptive mothers or mothers who undergo anesthesia, but for many women there are universal and defining moments during the delivery that help launch them into motherhood. The special events that take place during and right after delivery are like the tumblers of a lock falling into place one by one until the door into motherhood swings open.

AT THE LIMIT OF YOUR CAPACITIES

During labor, especially the last part, a woman instinctively knows she is performing one of the most vital tasks ever undertaken, and that lives are at stake, both hers and the baby's. What is happening at this moment is going on because of you, and in spite of you. It seems to carry all the power inherent in nature, whether of a rising tide or a cyclone. You have to go with the process so as to not lose yourself, and you have to be up to the task. There is no other choice. In these moments, you are stretched beyond all normal limits of concentration, endurance, pain, and purpose. The help of your husband and the midwife or nurse is invaluable, but you are still, in the most basic sense, on your own.

The extreme nature of this experience is what makes the act of delivering a baby a psychological transition, an event of trial and ritual that marks a profound change in your life. In spite of all this, in spite of the importance of the event, most mothers are too emptied, exhausted, quietly elated, relieved, and even disoriented to be able to grasp what the transition portends. But the events that follow will, one by one, fully reorganize and alter a new mother's world.

THE FIRST CRY

For many, the baby's first cry is like an alarm that awakens a whole new part of them. One mother said,

> I was used to feeling the baby inside me kicking and moving around, but she and I had a silent communication. I rubbed my belly a lot, and talked to her in my thoughts, but I hadn't really thought about her having a voice.
>
> When the baby came out and the midwife held her up before laying her on my stomach, she let out a little stuttering cry. I was stunned to hear her. It made her so real to me. She wasn't part of me anymore but had her own voice, and that meant she was her own little person.

For this mother, the first cry was what brought her the sudden realization that what had been one unit was now two.

LAYING THE BABY ON YOUR BELLY

According to long-standing custom, the person attending the birth will catch the baby, make a quick check to see that everything is all right, and then place the baby on the mother's belly for her to hold immediately and get to know. Like hearing the baby for the first time, for some mothers the weight and feel of the baby's body on top of theirs can be the powerful moment that crystallizes a piece of the motherhood mindset forever.

> After the baby came out I felt a huge relief that the pain had stopped, and I could finally let my body go. Then they put him on my belly, with his body warmth and aliveness, and I was overcome with a feeling of great completeness. His weight and form on me seemed to fill an emptiness along my body that I didn't even know was there till then. I felt a deep well-being. It was done. He was here on me. The circle was closed.

Holding the baby on top of you means another step has been taken. The baby has gone from the inside to the outside, but most mothers don't experience it exactly in those terms. At this point, the mother only knows she has done her job, the baby is alive, and she is back with her baby. The connection is different from what it was during pregnancy, but it is just as intimate.

Certain mothers are deprived of the experience of holding the baby against them right away because the baby has been whisked away for medical reasons and placed under surveillance in an isolette. It is only later, sometimes days later, when the baby is finally given to them to hold, that they realize the void they have been feeling, the need to hold the baby in their arms.

THE GAZE

Another key event for some mothers can be when the newborn first looks them in the eye, even for a moment. Right then, often with surprise and sharpness, mothers suddenly register what I call the baby's personhood.

Many newborns don't actually look around with clear eyes, but rather open their eyes in a fuzzy way that doesn't strike the mother so forcefully. They can do something else, however, that does have a strong effect. When the mother talks, they sometimes turn their head and eyes toward her face. Or if she moves her face, they sometimes follow with their gaze. In these small acts the mother feels that her baby knows her, has already chosen her, and has bonded with her. This knowledge moves her deeper into motherhood.

NURSING, AND A SHIFT
IN THE CENTER OF GRAVITY

The baby's first experience at the breast can bring its own delights or frustrations, but for many women it helps cement the fact that this is indeed her baby, and she is indeed the mother. *My baby came out crying and nursing. There was never a hesitation. I knew immediately that I was his mother. It was as if he knew, too.*

For others, nursing can be a series of missteps and false starts, resulting in a crying baby and a mother on the brink of despair. *The birth went fine, and Rosie was healthy, but she wasn't much interested in nursing. If I remember right, it was almost three days before we got it together and got the nursing going well. I was desperate, fearing we didn't go together or that I didn't have something she needed. I don't think we really bonded until that third day.*

Whether the nursing goes well right away or not, it signals another shift of perspective for the mother. During the pregnancy, and even immediately after the delivery, with the baby on her belly, the mother's emotional center of gravity remains concentrated on her womb and belly. That is where her physical center of gravity has been located for the many months of pregnancy. When the baby begins to nurse, however, the mother's center of emotional and physical gravity shifts up to her breasts and chest. Her breasts are where the all-important nursing takes place. And her chest is the place, now, where she will soothe her baby. It becomes the haven of safety for the baby and the source from which her physical love springs.

RECEPTIVITY AND ACTS OF PROTECTION

I can think of very few times in life when a woman is as vulnerable and impressionable as during the hours and days after the birth of her baby. It's as if she becomes a vibrant receptor field waiting for events to reveal themselves and take hold. She lies in a position of constructive fragility, taking in every nuance of what is said and done around her and the baby, even the most casual remarks.

After the baby is born, the new mother's sensitivity is compounded by the fact that everything happening around her falls on the richly worked mental terrain she has been nurturing for the last nine months. Remember, this is the moment when the real baby meets the imagined baby on the stage of her mind. In this light, a new mother is like a piece of psychologically fragile porcelain. Too often the medical staff does not realize how a casual remark or tone of concern can cause a hairline crack. "He is not the most active baby I've seen," the doctor may say to a new mother. Or to another doctor, "Check out the baby's heart for me again, we don't want to miss anything." These comments are like warning sirens to most new mothers, who are tuned to any indication that there could be a threat to the new baby.

In some situations, in spite of her fatigue, openness, and vulnerability, a new mother must act decisively to protect herself and her baby. She must follow her gut instincts, which can come as a surprise, even to her.

One woman had a very premature and difficult delivery. The medical complications were serious and immediate: the baby did not breathe right away and had to be assisted, and there was intracranial bleeding. When the doctor finally was able to put the little girl in her mother's arms, he described the situation to her tactfully but clearly. He explained that the delivery had been very hard on the baby and that he was obliged to tell her there was a real possibility that her baby could be blind as well as have some developmental delays. They talked for a bit, and then the doctor left the room. When he was gone, the mother looked down at her daughter and said tenderly, "Don't you listen to him, honey."

The mother was right to protect herself and the baby from an uncertain future. At the same time, the doctor was not wrong in telling her the possibilities. As it turned out, the little girl was perfectly normal by the age of one year. In a case like this, the woman's need to protect her newborn pushed her even faster into her motherhood identity.

CONTENTMENT

Far and away the most intense psychological impact of the birth for most women is the sense of accomplishment and completeness they feel after the event. Mothers describe feeling various mixtures of euphoria, exhaustion, depletion, victory, and relief. One mother described this situation: *I was in the shower right after the birth, washing off. Warm waves of happiness overcame me, and then I was crying. It was a shower of water, tears, and milk all running down me for a few minutes— like a tropical storm that appears overhead and moves on.*

Underlying this mixture of emotions is most often a profound sense of being part of the fertile earth, of being a member of the world, of belonging to eternity. At these moments, when the still exhausted mother is calm and the baby is in her arms, she may have an expression on her face that neither her husband nor friends have ever seen before, one they will never forget. There is none of the usual tension that keeps a face toned and ready to face the public. This face is rather private, quiet, and poised at a central still-point, full of a love without any external sign. This face has an unearthly beauty.

That is also how many mothers feel inside if they have been lucky in their birth experience. And if they have not, they may feel in some measure cheated. But even being cheated of some of the highs of the event will not stop their passage into the realm of motherhood.

The feeling of pure accomplishment that comes with the birth does a lot to give a woman confidence right from the beginning—when confidence is necessary. In short, you did it. Even if you needed medical assistance in the form of an epidural, spinal block, breaking the membranes, forceps, general anesthesia, or cesarean section, you still did it. You were successful in a situation that most likely felt out of your control. You were forced to trust your sensations and instincts and rely on your ability to tolerate pain and over-come physical challenges to perform an important feat. You carried a baby and delivered it successfully.

During labor and delivery, a couple may work together beautifully. This helps the woman include and trust her hus-band in his next role of supporting her as she learns to care for the baby. The success of going through it together stands you in good stead as a couple for the work still to come. In addition, as a new mother, you will have to come to grips with your need for the essential support and guidance, both practical and psychological, provided by medical staff and oftentimes by the midwife, nurses, and other mothers.

In summary, in the birth process the mother finishes most of the preparatory phase of her own birth as a mother. All the characters are now in place, and they have started to interact. As you hold the baby, touch her arms and legs, and gather her to your body, you make her your baby, and make yourself her mother. You have taken a giant step forward in your new identity and you are now almost ready to take on the even harder next phase that unfolds at home.

But first there is one more preparatory task to accomplish. And we turn to that next.

THREE

Self-fulfilling Prophecies and New Roles

To COMPLETE YOUR preparation for motherhood there is one more task to attend to, and again much of the work will take place in your mind. You have lived with an imaginary baby for the months of pregnancy, but around the time of the real baby's birth, mothers draw up mental blueprints for the future in which they assign specific identities and roles not only to their babies, but to their husbands and themselves.

Why do mothers choose this moment—the time of birth—to try to sketch a new plan for the future? It is because the entire preparatory phase that ends with the physical act of birthing has already significantly altered how they see themselves. Transformed into the mother of a child, with all the implications of closing out a long phase of your life, including your girlhood, you will find yourself poised at your baby's birth, facing at the same time an irrevocably lost past and an undefined future.

Having been brought up short in the course of their lives by this dramatic event, new mothers are forced to find new ways of living and, to some degree, new roles and functions for themselves and others. In spite of the changes, it is important to maintain the continuity of what you have known before. The result is a reshuffling in your mind of family roles and functions, using the same cards that have been in play all along: your husband, parents, siblings, and extended family. This metamorphosis during the postpartum weeks, which is steeped in feelings of closing the past, almost always invokes a current of sadness merging with the larger river of joyful feelings. Assigning imagined identities and roles, especially to your baby, is one way of coping with the perceived losses.

The roles and identities that you establish at this time set the direction for things to come. As a mother, you are making a prophecy as to which people will be in your life and what they will mean to you, and these prophecies are self-fulfilling. That is why it's so important to recognize this whole mental process. Your child and the rest of the family will have to live with the blueprints you design. They become guidelines for the future, but because they usually are developed unconsciously they are rarely thought through with care. Do the guidelines really represent the future you want? Your expectations and fantasies about your son or daughter can inspire the child to do great things, but they can hinder his development as well. It is worth becoming aware of what self-fulfilling prophecies you've set up for your family, and to recognize the potential benefits and risks for all concerned.

The process of prophesying and making blueprints continues after the birth of the baby as well as before. What happens is this. When you give birth, the imagined baby meets the real baby, but your imagined baby doesn't just disappear automatically. It will reassert itself, though it will be revised a bit to adjust to the realities of sex, size, appearance, coloration, and temperament. The updated version of the imaginary baby continues to live in your mind alongside the real one. You continue to look at your real baby through the lens of your wishes, dreams, and fears. There is the baby in your arms, and the one in your mind, and they are rarely exactly the same.

One woman looking back at her first months as a new mother was perceptive enough to see that she had often been frustrated, and she was then able to identify part of the reason for this.

> I don't think I really enjoyed the first few months of motherhood at all. I was always on edge, waiting for the next cry from baby Lisa. It seemed like all she did was cry, and fuss, and arch her back. I was so looking forward to being a mother, but it wasn't anywhere near as fun as I had anticipated. I was actually beginning to think we made a big mistake in having a baby at all.
>
> Finally Doug and I talked about it because he could see my frustration level getting dangerously high. Talking with Doug made me realize something pretty important. It sounds silly, but my dream baby, the one I thought about when I was pregnant, was a little peach of a child, lying

peacefully in my arms as the sunlight streamed in the window, and the birds sang in the background.

The real baby Lisa is not a peach. She's a tiger, and she never lies peacefully in anybody's arms. When I finally admitted to myself that I had a fussy baby instead of a peaceful one, I was able to deal with it better. There wouldn't be quiet moments in the sunlight with Lisa, but there would be exciting ones. No one will ever say Lisa is boring.

In a similar way, most new mothers carry a mental image of themselves as a mother, which is often different from the reality. You may have worried about sleeping through the baby's cry in the middle of the night because you're such a sound sleeper, and then in fact find that you wake up immediately every time. Again, you will find yourself looking at your life through a lens of your fears and wishes, which separates the real from the imagined. For some women the real mother turns out to be the better one; for others this isn't so. All mothers, however, have to deal with the power of their expectations in comparison to reality, and how they apply these expectations to their husbands, the baby, and to themselves.

THE IMAGINED BABY
FULFILLING THE MOTHER'S NEEDS

All mothers expect their babies to fulfill some of their personal needs, ambitions, and wishes and, conversely, to repair some of their failures and disappointments. I would like to describe for you the most common blueprints women construct in their minds concerning the baby-to-come and its imagined role in their life.

Unconditional Love

Before actually becoming a mother, most women wonder how it will be to love their babies and, just as important, how their babies will love them. Many people in our society feel that when it comes to their own childhood, they did not receive unconditional love from their parents: they were loved for what they did, not for who they were. To maintain their parents' love, they felt driven to be good in school, or popular socially, or successful in business, or athletically gifted, or musically accomplished, or whatever their parents felt was important. Those were the conditions of being well loved.

A woman with this in her background might hope that with the birth of her own child she will finally have someone who will love her no matter what. The very idea can be deeply satisfying and feel like a kind of reparation. However, it can also make it hard on this mother at those inevitable times when the baby is angry at her and rejects her, or simply starts to become more independent as a natural part of maturation.

A mother described having these feelings when she looked at her daughter for the first time. It's easy to see how this mother's past dictates the role she wants her baby to play.

My family was all wrong. We were four sisters, a crazy mother, and totally quiet father. Emotions ruled the day in our household, and we still can't talk to each other without falling into the old patterns of arguing, martyrdom, and then cutting each other off. Most of it came from my mother. She taught us all how to inflict hurt, specially with people you are supposed to love.

When I struggled into a sitting position in that hospital and the doctor put my daughter in my arms, I tell you, I looked down at her and in my heart I knew this was the person who would always be there for me, who would understand me and not close herself off from me. I wouldn't let her.

The Replacement Baby

When a woman has suffered the loss of a loved one prior to the birth of her child, she may understandably see the baby as a replacement of the beloved in some way. This urge is even stronger if the loss occurred during the pregnancy, but it can have occurred years before and still be strong. Diana, near the end of her pregnancy, thought about an aunt who was very dear to her in this way.

At the airport today with so much snow on the ground, I was reminded of last winter when I flew to see Aunt Claudia for the last time. I remembered waiting for that flight with all the travelers with heavy coats on, knowing that I was going to her house just to say good-bye.

The older I get, the more I'm amazed by what she did for me. I was just ten when I went to stay with her. Ten-year-olds look little to me now, but when I was ten, I thought I was so mature. Everything had been difficult with my mother. I was in the same house with her but she seemed miles away, and she was always crying or going into her bedroom. The house seemed empty. When she said I was going to stay with Aunt Claudia for a while, I remember thinking I would do it if it made things better.

When I first saw Claudia's house, back then, I thought it was a giant mess. Now I realize it was lived in. She was plunk in the middle of living, with papers, and books, and phone messages, and a dog that slept on the couch when she wasn't looking, and leftovers in the refrigerator because she really cooked.

From the first day Claudia included me. She worked at a desk in her room sometimes, but didn't go to a job every day. Mostly she visited friends, helped out at the library, took care of two elderly ladies, sisters, who lived next door, and weeded the garden, her own as well as other people's. And she took me with her everywhere as if I belonged. Those eight months were like living in color after so many years of living in black and white, alone with my mother.

I don't like to think she's gone. That last trip was hard, when we both knew it was the end. Then, two months after the funeral, I got pregnant, and the minute I found out it was a girl, I knew right away I would name her Claudia. I suppose that's the way these things happen—death and life come really close together sometimes. I thought then, and I sometimes still think, Oh Claudia, what am I going to do with a baby?

When the lost person is a parent or someone else very close, there is a tendency (often supported by religious custom) to keep the memory of that person alive by naming the baby after him or her. What also happens is that the new parent sometimes wants and needs the baby to take up some of the meaning for them that the lost person had. This was certainly true for Diana, who hoped for a baby girl who would be full of life and would help bring color to her own world.

Sometimes fulfilling this replacement role can create a huge burden for the new baby, who is being asked to fill someone else's shoes when it is scarcely clear to the parents, let alone the baby, that this is their assignment in life.

Sometimes the lost person can be a miscarried or stillborn baby, or a baby who died of sudden infant death syndrome. Under these circumstances, especially when the parents know the sex and other facts about the lost baby, it is hard for them to avoid expecting the new baby to play a role in filling the loss, to inherit the dreams and fantasies that had been inspired by the other baby. This is not necessarily a bad thing unless the new baby lives in the persistent shadow of the one whom the parent is still mourning.

The Baby as an Antidepressant

New mothers often get depressed for varying stretches of time as they adjust to life with a baby. And there are mothers who deal with a lifelong tendency toward depression, which doesn't go away when the baby arrives. In these situations it may happen that the mother, without realizing it, uses the baby to keep her animated and involved in life; in short, to act like an antidepressant.

Since childhood Diana tended to get depressed. When she was a girl she always had a best girlfriend who was vivacious and outgoing, the risk taker who pushed Diana into adventures and social encounters, virtually forcing her into life. There was always a friend who revitalized her when she started to sink emotionally.

This is what Diana's Aunt Claudia could do for her that her own mother could not. She had a succession of antidepressant girlfriends in high school and after. Her husband, Carl, performs that important function for her from time to time, but he is not always successful. Diana's fantasy, which she was usually unaware of, was that the baby would play the role of an antidepressant and reanimator. This fantasy was in opposition to another one that she was aware of, namely, that the baby would be placid and easy.

Being the assigned antidepressant for the mother can be a heavy responsibility for an infant. And to fill it, the baby may have to become (if her temperament allows it) very active or charming. But what if little Claudia turns out to be placid and quiet?

The Vicarious Baby

Inevitably our children are extensions of ourselves stretching into the future. All parents have unfulfilled dreams, journeys not taken, paths they have ignored. The desire to repair or redo your own past vicariously through your child is understandable. So you end up believing it would be a good idea for your daughter to take ballet classes, or your son to study more, even when that is not necessarily their wish, nor in their best long-term interests. The rehearsal of an imaginary future for your baby may include replaying your own real past.

Just as often you want for your baby some of the experiences that were the most successful and gratifying for you.

Whenever we see unusual career successes occurring in two or more generations, there is probably a confluence of a genetic gift enhanced by a facilitating fantasy.

Although it is a well known fact that parents try to live vicariously through their children, it is often hard to see this tendency in ourselves, and even when we do, we often underestimate how powerful an impact it has on the child.

THE IMAGINED BABY'S EFFECT ON YOUR MARRIAGE

All new mothers wonder about the impact the baby will have on their marriage. It is unavoidable that there will be an impact. With one act, two people become three, a couple becomes a family. The adjustments are momentous and unpredictable. Women may hold several ideas about the possible consequences the arrival of a baby will have on their marriage.

Marital Glue or Marital Threat

Some mothers, and fathers as well, hope their new baby will act as a kind of marital glue to hold the marriage together forever. With the birth of the baby, they think, neither the husband nor the wife will be able to leave.

Hiding behind this imagined role for the baby may be very real fears of a broken marriage. Perhaps one of the parents has divorced parents. Or perhaps there remain important unresolved questions about the future of this marriage. And what if, later on, it turns out that the baby fails in its assigned role and the marriage falls apart anyway? How fair is it to ascribe this role of savior to your child?

Still other women imagine the opposite; that the baby will threaten the harmony or exclusivity of their marriage. Such concerns can be fleeting thoughts or they can become preoccupations. If the baby is seen in this light, there are really only two views the mother can take. Either the fragile marriage must be protected from the disrupting baby, and the baby pushed to the periphery. Or the baby must be protected from the marriage, and the marriage pushed to the periphery. In either scenario, a destructive competition gets set up in which either the baby or the marriage suffers—or, most likely, both.

The Baby as Competition

Whereas some mothers worry that the coming baby will ruin their companionship with their husbands, others focus specifically on how they think their husband will react to having a new baby in the house. They may expect their husbands to enfold the baby completely. It can be disconcerting to such a mother, to say the least, to find herself with a husband who not only doesn't want to embrace the baby but in addition is jealous of it and feels that his needs are no longer being met and that he no longer has his wife's attention. This often leads to a syndrome in which the husband becomes a "second baby": Dad demands Mom's attention and if he isn't satisfied with the response (and he rarely is because she is dealing with a very real other baby), he moves out of the marriage emotionally, usually to lose himself in work.

Even in the best cases, couples can feel they have lost something of the couple dynamic when their baby is born. In a sense they have lost a certain exclusivity. In most cases this sense of loss is short term, and as the new family emerges, a healthy new balance emerges as well. On the other hand, some mothers do become overinvolved in the baby to the exclusion of other roles, including that of wife, in which case the husband's jealousy is understandable.

In the period immediately following the birth of the baby, the way the man acts as a father to the baby and as a husband to his wife goes a long way toward determining how his wife will come to view him over the coming years as a partner and as a man. This is a long-term process, but often the future course of your marriage starts to be set around these issues. Resentments that begin at this time can fester for years, so it's vitally important for the two of you to explore these issues with honesty and commitment.

Imagining the Perfect Family

Some women want to believe that their new baby will lift their marriage to higher levels of harmony and satisfaction. They want the baby's arrival to result in an idealized triad, the perfect family. In this fantasy, the real baby is saddled with a lot of baggage that really belongs to the imagined baby. What actually constitutes the perfect family? Is it one child? Three? Four? Ten? Most often this magic number comes from the family of origin. If your nuclear family consisted of five members and your new family only of three, you may feel a vague sense of failure or incompleteness. The danger, of course, arises when you give the imagined ideal more importance than the real needs of the individuals involved.

When there already is a child in the family, the next baby may be valued less as herself than as the needed sibling for the first child. Here, too, the parents' personal histories play a big role—and much of this is perfectly understandable. For instance, if you hated being an only child, why wouldn't you try to avoid making your own firstborn an only child? The key to avoiding such traps is to become aware of your thought process. Until you address these fantasies, it's hard for you to appreciate your real baby for who he really is.

The Baby as a Carrier of Flaws

Often parents perceive particular faults in their spouses or in members of the spouse's family, or even in themselves and their own families. The perceived fault might be a seemingly small thing like wearing thick glasses, being short, talking too slowly, having a big nose or a darker complexion, or being too extroverted or too shy. These traits have a way, however, of being stubbornly annoying, so much so that they come to represent more important perceived failures in the partner. Naturally, the mother's expectation is that her baby will not share these qualities. But if she does, the tendency may be to blame the parent who passed on the trait.

Even a presumably good quality can be seen as negative or threatening. Consider the problem Ellen had with her own reactions when people commented on her son's attractiveness.

I have two absolutely beautiful children, and God knows I'm doing the best I can to raise them alone. Their father walked out on me for a younger woman when he turned forty, just like his father did. The men in this family have a real womanizing problem.

Anyway, whenever someone looks at little Jim and comments on how charming and handsome he is, I feel an icy hand on my heart. I will not let this little boy grow up to be a charmer. He will not continue the family pattern.

The Baby as a Gift

Many cultures believe that a woman is a failure as a wife if she cannot produce the gift of a son for her husband. This idea is not a dominant one in the modern West, but there are other ways that a baby can be viewed as a gift, and many of these ideas can be problematic. For instance, suppose the wife is approaching forty and wants to have a child before it's too late, but the husband is reluctant. He doesn't feel ready, and in fact doesn't know whether he ever will be. They don't have the luxury of many more years to work out their differences. Let's say he finally acquiesces. The baby then becomes something he has done for her, a sort of gift. Will she at some later date have to pay a price for this gift? If so, how long will the installments last? Will the baby have to pay too?

On the other hand, imagining the baby as a gift can be seen in a positive light. This can happen with couples who have been trying for a very long time to have a baby and finally do. Such couples often see their babies as a gift from God.

I have seen very religious couples who, upon learning that they will give birth to a handicapped baby, also interpret this as a gift from God. Such couples can make wonderful parents for such babies. Their viewpoint, that raising this baby is a way to do God's work, permits them to dwell on the positive and not be paralyzed by the drawbacks. It makes their task of helping the baby reach his full potential far easier and less full of anguish.

THE IMAGINED BABY AND THE FAMILY'S DESTINY

Parents generally invest their babies with their hopes for the future. As soon as the baby arrives, the existing structure of grandparents, aunts, uncles, cousins, parents, brothers, and sisters must shift to make room, even a specific place, for the new family member. This shift brings into relief a dream of the future, a dream of the next generation and what it might mean for us, its forebears. These expectations place a significant burden on the child and need to be examined.

An Agent for Social Mobility

When people move to a new country or region or even a new neighborhood, they feel like immigrants. After all, it takes three or so generations for a family to establish roots and have a history in a new locale—to feel as though they truly belong.

Without realizing it fully, some new parents believe that their babies will change the course of their personal destinies. Deep down they might think that if their child grows up to attend the right schools, make a lot of money, speak without an accent, or marry well, it will enhance the whole family's position—all of which may be true. These aspirations are most often unspoken, but in terms of the effect they have on the child, they come through loud and clear. As a parent, you can miss entire aspects of your child's personality or innate talents because they do not advance the family's social aims. For instance, if a boy is dreamy, poetic, and sensitive, but those traits aren't seen as assets for the purpose of upward mobility, they may be minimized or discouraged. Instead, the talents that will effect change, such as being outgoing and assertive, will get strongly reinforced.

One of the most important and difficult tasks of parenting is to allow the child to become her own person. To reinforce only the traits that serve your dreams as opposed to your child's is a pit even the most well-intentioned parents fall into. Certainly not all of the ramifications show up when the child is an infant, but it is never too early to think about what we are unfairly projecting onto our children.

Throughout history it has been said that the first generation in a new land has to be soldiers so that the next generation can be farmers, so that the next generation can be professionals, so that the following generation can be artists and scientists. The baby that the family wants and needs for its own goals or place in history can shape the future of the real baby for better or worse.

I have spent much time working in New York and in Geneva. Both cities have a strong tradition of immigration, but throughout the world migration is becoming more and more prevalent, and it is practically ubiquitous within the United States, with its great geographic mobility. Since the process of putting down roots takes several generations, only a minority of families escape the influence of migration. It inspires one of the most pervasive fantasies influencing how we shape our children.

The Weight of Family Traditions

Some babies may be expected to maintain family traditions. For instance, if the baby boy is the third generation of first sons, all of whom are lawyers practicing in the family firm, he will have to fight very hard not to fulfill his projected family destiny. It could be the same in a family of athletes, bankers, union workers, churchgoers, or beekeepers. These traditional family roles can have enormous power in shaping a child's future. They act like huge gravitational fields, controlling almost all elements of the family's daily life: what the parents present as a model for the child and what she learns to imitate, what the parents choose to teach, topics of family interest and dinner-table conversation, the overt and covert transmission of values, the choice of family friends and recreational activities. Generally speaking, these forces are so strong that children either accept them and conform, escape through rebellion, or find a neutral third path, but chances are they will still constantly be reminded of the extent to which they have deviated from the collective family fantasy.

The Imagined Conciliator

If Romeo and Juliet had lived and had a baby, would the birth of their child have made peace between the families?

Some parents hope that the birth of their baby will soften the hearts of their own parents who may not have approved of their marriage or even refused to go to the wedding. Scott's wife tells the story of her imagined baby.

My dad and I have always been very close, and I guess you could say that no man I chose to marry would have been good enough for me. I've always idolized my dad as well. When I brought home Scott, I brought Dad close to a heart attack. Our family is very white, and Scott is a black American.

It's been awful for about two years now. Conversations with my father are short and strained, and I know he only comes to visit when my mother makes him. Now, however, we're going to have a baby, and we know it's a girl. Over and over again I picture myself driving up my parents' driveway, getting out of the car, and bringing our baby to the front door. When my father opens the door, I just hand her to him. What can he do? He takes her and holds her rigidly. Then, he stops looking at me and looks down at her. She melts his heart.

While the scenario could unfold in exactly this way, imagine the opposite. What if this perfectly fine newborn girl, ready to be loved, profoundly disappoints her parents because the grandfather doesn't respond to her? Unknowingly, this child will already have failed at one of the fantasized reasons for her being—to reconcile mother and grandfather. Surely this burden is too heavy for anyone, much less an infant, to bear.

Margaret, the woman who takes a middle-view perspective on her family, offers a less extreme version of this same issue. The relationship between her parents and her in-laws had always been cordial, but lukewarm, in part because of the religious and social differences between them. Margaret hopes the baby-to-come will bridge the distance so that she will feel accepted and her time with Jim's family can feel more natural. Here is Margaret's expression of her imagined baby.

I have never fit in well at Jim's family gatherings, and last night was as uncomfortable as always. They are so different from my family. Everyone there is louder somehow, and I honestly think they need to have more than one person talking at the same time to feel like it's a real conversation.

Thank God my parents weren't there last night. The wedding reception was bad enough with Jim's part of the room drinking and dancing, and little pockets of my family sitting quietly at their tables trying to talk. I'm always in the middle trying to defend each side to the other, and I'm not very good at it. Jim never tries to defend, but I know he wants me to like his family more than I do.

I do like his parents and his brothers and sisters, but I don't know how to act around them. Last night was so typical. I was sitting in the middle of three conversations, but nothing was coming out of my mouth. Everyone else was funny and I felt like the ice queen. I know I looked like I was being snobby, but I wasn't. I just don't know how to relate easily there. I remember thinking, "Oh please, don't let them play games after supper." I bet Jim wonders why I can't go along with the flow like everyone else. I felt like telling everyone I had to go to bed. I'm so big with this baby, they wouldn't be able to argue.

When the baby comes I think . . . hope things will

change. All the attention will be on the baby and not on me anymore. Jim's parents will love having a newborn around again, and maybe I'll finally look real in their eyes because I've given them a new family member. Wouldn't it be amazing if Jim's parents and my parents were in the same room with the baby, and we all got along? And we all felt easy? What a picture that would be. This baby will have to be very diplomatic to keep both sides of the family happy. That shouldn't be hard for a baby. All it has to do is be cute and smile.

Diana, who maintains a more distant view of her mother, long ago gave up on her parents' power to play any role in legitimizing or even influencing her marriage, let alone anything else in her life. Diana, unlike Margaret, did not have any reparative fantasies or daydreams. For her such ideas were not conceivable and maybe not even desirable.

The wishes and fears about the two families of origin getting together around the child touches a deep chord in the marriage. New parents have to establish their own nuclear family and give it a certain priority. This means that a distance between them and their parents must be established and maintained, if it hasn't been already. For Diana, this will prove to be a very easy task, but for Emily (the "close-up view" mother) it will be problematic. You can already see the conflict for Emily in a dream she had several months after the baby was born.

It was a very confusing dream. There was my mother, my grandmother, my sister, me, and a baby. And we were all at a bath house at the beach, showering. But everyone kept changing ages. So at one point my grandmother was the young woman with the baby. And the baby was . . . I don't know . . . me? My daughter? My mother? And I and my mother were older and were watching. Then it shifted again and my sister and I were girls at the beach and I was wearing an old-fashioned one-piece bathing suit from the twenties, all black, while someone else was taking care of the baby. It was weird. We were having a good time, but, I don't know, something was unsettling.

In Emily's dream it is hard to tell where one generation leaves off and the next begins. And, indeed, this will be an issue for her. She imagines that she and the new baby will automatically remain in the bosom of her family. She is not yet aware of any of the possible tensions that will arise in defining herself not as a daughter but as a mother in her own right, nor has she reflected much on the place of her new nuclear family within her family of origin. Her baby-to-be thus has no imagined role to play here. At a later point, after the baby is born and some natural tensions do arise among her different roles in the family, she will have to be careful not to attribute to the baby the imaginary role of creating interference between her and her original family.

The Role in the Family Mythology

Families build myths about themselves that are necessary to help structure people's lives together. The baby-to-be may be assigned a certain role in one of these family myths or dramas. For instance, when there have been serious feuds in different branches of the family, one family branch may need a "family avenger"—someone who will right the ancient wrongs, reestablish the family's former place, or replenish the lost family fortune.

In most extended families there are inequalities among the different branches. For instance, the uncle, who was the firstborn and favorite of the grandparents, and his wife and all his children may be considered better or more special than the family of his younger brother. These differences in stature are recognized by all, but usually never talked about except at moments of family crisis. It is hard for the younger brother's family not to fantasize about having a baby who turns out to be so extraordinary as an athlete, celebrity, genius, or business tycoon that it would guarantee them a place in the sun.

There are other roles, many passed on for generations, that people in the family tend to fall into to keep the whole structure in equilibrium. In some families there is always a black sheep, a beautiful but sinful femme fatale, a great hope who will nevertheless fail, the family sage, the hero, the family savior, the family confidant, the family "newspaper" (to whom all family members speak privately, knowing well it will be repeated for all to hear), the family's emotional centerpiece who holds everyone together, the family jester, or the family swizzle stick who keeps everyone in animated contact. There is often an unconscious tendency to guide members of the younger generation into fulfilling one of these roles.

If the circumstances are right—the slot is empty, the sex of the baby is appropriate—the new child will be viewed as following in so-and-so's footsteps. It sometimes takes great effort to break out of these family stereotypes and allow the baby to establish a unique identity.

There are many more imaginary babies made up from the mix of your fantasies, wishes, fears, and past history: the baby as a playmate, as the love of your life, as a reflection of you, as proof of your femininity or creativity, as a completion of you as a whole person, as the fantasized child of a lost lover, and so on. It is important to stress that all of these imaginary babies are normal constructions of the mind as it strives to come to grips with one of the transformative events of your life. Unattended and carried too far, the imagined babies can create problems and push your real child into roles either too heavy or inappropriate to bear.

Recognizing that you have a mental blueprint in place is important because once you are conscious of it you can then decide to avoid or fulfill it. You can put it to good use in helping your child recognize his own best internal design and realize it, but in addition, you need to know how to put it aside and see who your baby really is. The baby and family you imagine become a self-fulfilling prophecy. It is up to you to recognize your blueprint and decide if it is really what you want for your child.

The formation of these ideals brings to a close the preparation phase of the development of your motherhood identity. We now have in place a real baby, a mother and father, and a blueprint for the future in the form of imagined roles and functions. We now proceed to your actual birth as a mother, where the basic tasks of motherhood will finally forge your identity.

PART II

A Mother Is Born

FOUR

Ensuring Your Baby's Survival

A S SOON AS you arrive home with your new baby, you encounter the basic tasks of parenting whether you feel ready or not. All mothers must struggle with the basics and succeed; the baby must live and must thrive. This encounter with your primary responsibility as a parent finally gives psychological birth to your new identity. It is in the act of fulfilling these new responsibilities that you finally really become a mother.

The first, unavoidable task of motherhood is to keep your baby alive. Within minutes you are called upon to ensure the physical survival and growth of your offspring. As a society we tend to forget this obvious and stark reality, to take for granted the drama and import of the task, but it doesn't go unnoticed in a mother's heart. Living with your new baby, you will constantly face the realization that a fragile life depends on you, and wonder whether you will be able not only to keep him alive but to help him grow.

Why is this your foremost task, and why is it so charged with purpose? Survival of the individual and his or her genes (in the form of offspring) is the greatest responsibility nature imposes on all animals. This is the drive behind our need to reproduce and propagate the species. All of our biological and psychological theories propose that to assure this, we as human animals are endowed with instincts which guarantee that our genes will get handed down to the next generation.

First we are endowed with self-preservation instincts so that we can stay alive long enough to reproduce. Then we have social instincts that permit us to get into a relationship with someone of the opposite sex so that courting and reproduction can take place. And of course we are equipped with the well-known sexual instincts that ensure the continuation of the species.

Suppose that all of these instinctual processes succeed. Then what? We have a baby—the final fruit. But our lifelong instincts would be in vain if we weren't equipped with encoded instructions for how to care for the child until her own survival instincts kick in and start to play an appreciable role in her life. As a mother, you automatically provide an essential link in evolution's precious chain. A mother with her fears and fatigue and banal daily acts of protecting the baby and providing care is playing a central role in nature's grand design.

So far, what I've described is theory, but it gets lived at the very real level of a mother's daily experience with her baby. Part of what makes the experience of motherhood so singular is that it forces a woman to become preoccupied with entirely new concerns, moving her to act under the guidance of new impulses that she has never before experienced.

The startling reality of the responsibility for their baby's survival strikes most mothers with enormous force. Despite medical and family backup and the fact that a portion of the caregiving task is shared by your husband, the culture has nominated you, the mother, as the responsible guardian. If anything goes wrong, chances are the ultimate responsibility will fall to you. This reality is the single most compelling raw fact of a new mother's experience.

For some, the realization comes while they're still in the hospital, postpartum. For others, it comes a week or so later after the nurse or their own mother goes back home. The impact of this new reality may get triggered at completely ordinary moments: holding the baby and feeling how small and vulnerable she is, or watching her sleep and seeing her tiny chest cage rise and fall. But no matter when it dawns on you, the realization of this awesome responsibility will change your world forever.

Let us look more closely at these first responsibilities and the concerns that accompany them.

KEEPING YOUR BABY ALIVE

The first and strongest concern of a new mother is whether her baby will stop breathing. On the first nights home, and often for some time after, this concern sends a new mother to the side of her sleeping baby over and over again. You may joke about it the next morning, but the urgency that sends you to the baby's bedside is powerful, preemptive, deadly serious, and cannot be ignored without enormous anxiety.

One mother whose sister's baby recently died of sudden infant death syndrome told me after her own baby arrived:

> At the baby's birth, we got a baby monitor to hear exactly what went on in the baby's room, maybe because of what happened to my sister. I remember putting the baby down for a nap and taking the monitor into the kitchen. I don't think of myself as a worrier, but unconsciously I must have been keeping track of his breathing, because all of a sudden when I didn't hear him, or if his breathing was in any way irregular, I would run up the stairs and check on him. Time after time I found myself in his room with my hand on his back to feel him breathe, or with my ear next to his face to hear the breaths. Sometimes it was hard to hear him because I was breathing so hard from running up the stairs.

Most new mothers fear that the baby will die or be hurt through carelessness or inadequacy. Have you never worried that the baby will fall from the changing table onto its head when you are not looking; or that the baby will slip out of your wet and soapy hands and drown in the bath? Or maybe he'll bang his head on the tub when you take him out, or get tangled up in the blankets or get caught under a pillow and suffocate? You've also probably worried when the baby is lying in bed with you, that your husband or you will roll over and crush her arm, or that she will get overheated from too many clothes and blankets, or that she is not dressed warmly enough and will freeze during the night, particularly if the window is left open.

These are the natural fears that keep new mothers vigilant, the better to protect their babies and at the same time help them internalize and absorb their new responsibilities. These worries can manifest themselves in odd ways, such as a strong concern over who is allowed to hold or touch the baby. It is natural for you as the person who is ultimately responsible for this little being to become very alert to your feelings about whether someone is safe for your baby or could possibly pose a threat. It may surprise you when these feelings override your usual politeness toward relatives and friends. Your decision about who can join the small circle of people whom you allow to hold the baby is based on the sense of security they inspire in you, not on how closely they are related. This largely intuitive judgment can sometimes create tricky problems within the family.

One mother recalled this incident:

> We have a friend of the family who talks a lot and fidgets nervously with her hands. Her husband is a big deal in town, so people treat her politely, even though she's hard to be around. Well, she came over when I was visiting my mother, and wanted to hold the baby. Mom was holding him, and passed him over to Mrs. Morse. The baby looked up at her with his big eyes and then wrinkled his face and began to cry. She started jiggling him and saying "You mustn't cry. You mustn't cry."
>
> "He's hungry," I snapped, and snatched him from her arms to take him in the other room. It was totally rude, but I didn't care. I didn't want that woman holding my baby.

Being preoccupied almost to the point of obsession about protecting your baby is perfectly understandable, even when there is only a slight chance of risk. Most women find there is no precedent in their lives for the fierceness of their love and concern for their children.

When my baby was three weeks old, I put her in a front sack and walked up the street to get lunch. We live in the city and the sidewalks were crowded with people rushing around. At the corner I paused for the light to change and then stepped out into the street. People were coming toward us from the opposite direction. One man caught my eye. He was moving fast and suddenly seemed to veer directly toward me. I thought he was going to crash into the baby. Instantly both my arms were in front of my chest ready to protect my daughter and grab the man by the throat. In a flash he passed me and was gone. So much emotion raced through me in about three seconds, including being ready to kill if necessary.

These fearful thoughts are inevitable. In the inexperienced eyes of a mother who holds the final responsibility for survival, a newborn appears fragile and vulnerable. Only with experience do you realize how robust newborns really are. During my first years of medical school I learned about all the things that could go wrong and all the possible illnesses that one could contract. It seemed a miracle that anyone could actually stay alive for a lifetime. In the next few years, when I left the classroom and began to have clinical experiences, it seemed even more amazing to me how resistant, tough, and well adapted the human body is. Illness and death have a real fight on their hands with the robust design of the human being, but for a new mother it is hard to appreciate this.

Fears for the baby's survival lessen with time, but they never fully go away. They simply move into the background of your concerns. They also transform appropriately to fit the child's age. The mother of a two-year-old who gets into everything may worry that he will strangle himself with a cord or put his finger in the electric socket, while the mother of a preteen will worry about kidnappers or traffic accidents. Some level of fearfulness always remains latent, ready to be revived when circumstances demand it.

MAKING YOUR BABY GROW AND THRIVE

A second group of major concerns has to do with whether you will succeed in making the baby gain weight and stay healthy. The sorts of questions all new mothers ask themselves are, Do I know how to nurse well enough? Will I have enough milk? Will I know when the baby has had enough to eat? Can I read the baby's signals so that the feeding goes well? Is there a good enough fit between the shape of my nipple and the shape of the baby's mouth? Might the baby be allergic to my milk? Is my milk flowing so fast that he might choke, or too slowly so that he is frustrated? Will my baby become dehydrated? Will he have to go back to the hospital? These kinds of questions arise whether you are breast- or bottle-feeding your baby. They will resurface yet again when the baby is ready to eat solid food.

In the case of feeding, as with his physical survival, you

are pulled and pushed by forces over which you have little control. First, there is your heightened responsiveness to the baby's signals (his incessant crying or his captivating smile). You can't dampen your sensitivity to these signals or turn down the volume. You are a captive audience of your own finely tuned sensibilities. Then there are the innate urges and acts that you perform, such as holding the baby's head, caressing her in a certain way, or facing her to the breast, and, finally, there are the powerful expectations that society imposes on you, and that you adopt for yourself. When all of these are working together it is little wonder that you get up at any hour of the night, on any schedule, for weeks on end, regardless of how exhausted you are. Don't be surprised if your days are constructed around the baby's feeding and sleeping schedule, no matter what else is going on around you. It makes sense in a profound way that everything concerning feeding and weight gain is loaded with import and emotion. After all, a baby's continued survival depends on making sure she's growing.

One mother recounted:

When my son was just a week old, he began to lose weight. The doctor's voice sounded concerned as he told me the baby had to grow. That sent me into a panic. The more I panicked, the less milk I seemed to have, and soon he fell back to his birth weight. This caused even more alarm at the doctor's office, and they made me supplement with formula. I've never felt so helpless. I held on to that baby for dear life, thinking about feeding him, trying to feed him, burping him, and constantly wondering how much he weighed.

When he spit up for the first time, I was horrified.

Maybe he couldn't eat, and would just pine away. They called it failure to thrive, and all I could think about was getting this baby to gain weight. I'm the kind of woman who always had my hair and clothes looking nice, but during this time period, I didn't care what I looked like. I walked around in the same clothes day after day, just holding my son. When he finally hit eight pounds I broke down and wept in the doctor's office. Nothing mattered in life except this baby eating.

It is not surprising that apparently simple decisions about whether to breast- or bottle-feed, or whether to supplement feedings, often become completely charged with emotion. For the same reason, seemingly insignificant comments from your mother like "Well, he isn't very chubby, is he?" or "Why aren't her cheeks fatter?" land on fertile soil. While you may try to laugh them off, they strike at the heart of your most pressing concern, and you can't help hearing this kind of remark as a profound reproach of your abilities as a mother. At times, these comments leave scars or start family battles that may not be patched over for years. What is at stake is too vital. Any signals that undermine your confidence while you are trying to do something you have never done before are upsetting and not to be borne.

One mother found herself questioning her confidence in an almost ridiculous series of events one afternoon soon after she gave birth to her daughter.

When I first started taking my baby daughter out on errands, I carried her in a front sack. On the first warm day of the year, we went out, and I was so thrilled to be in the sunshine with my new baby. In the library, a woman I didn't know came up to me. "Excuse me," she said, "but don't you know your baby can catch cold? Get some socks on that baby right now." I was so flustered, I immediately dug around for her socks and pulled them on her little feet.

Later in the day as I headed home, I stood on the sidewalk waiting to cross. I was growing used to people staring at the baby and smiling, but one man nearby seemed to take great interest in her. Finally he leaned over toward me and said, "I can see this is your first baby. Better get those socks off her now. It's way too hot for socks." Flustered again, I tugged them off her feet before crossing the street.

Once in our apartment, I felt safe from strangers giving me advice. I put the baby down on my bed for a nap and walked into the next room. She was crying, but I knew she would fall asleep if left alone for a few minutes. Then I heard a new sound, like someone tapping on the bedroom window. It was impossible. Our apartment is on the fourth floor. Rushing back into the bedroom, I was astonished to see a man balanced on a board outside the bedroom window with a paintbrush in his hand. Holding the paintbrush with one hand, he was tapping on my window with the other.

When he saw me come into the bedroom, his face stretched into a big smile and he pointed at my baby. "Your baby is crying," he mouthed through the window, pleased that he could alert me to the situation. I almost cried myself. Was I so incapable of caring for this child that people needed to scale the apartment walls and hang in space to tell me what to do?

AM I A NATURALLY ENDOWED MOTHER?

To be ultimately responsible for your baby's survival and growth resonates with such power because it speaks to the fundamental question: Will I succeed as a human animal, that is, an organism so exquisitely designed by nature that it can reproduce and continue the survival of the species? Of course you don't walk around quizzing yourself in those words, but the question underlies many of a new mother's daily uncertainties.

Are you then a naturally endowed animal? Are you capable of bringing along the next generation and propagating the family's genes? There are not many bigger questions than these. And although it is rarely discussed in these terms, it is perfectly clear to all concerned (you, your husband, your family) that underneath everything, this is what is at stake. You are being tested at this most basic level of biological functioning and must prove that you can perform competently.

When you are in the throes of new motherhood, you can't consciously think in terms of these broad questions. You would probably explode. Nonetheless they will be in the background driving you to act according to some standard you never even thought about before, a standard whose origin you cannot even identify. This is an awesome responsibility.

In our world, to fail in the workplace is bad enough. To fail as a social human being is devastating. But to fail as a human animal is almost unthinkable. Many new mothers marvel that mammals like dogs and cats or deer in the wild know what to do. They desperately hope that they, too, are naturally endowed with these same animal instincts to keep their baby alive and well. They know they are likely to run into situations where what they have learned before will not suffice, and they will have to reach into some unlearned reservoir of parental intuition that had better be there, and had better be full enough.

A DIFFERENT LOOK AT A MOTHER'S FEAR

The fears for the baby's survival and growth, and for your adequacy as a human animal are not only normal but necessary. They serve an important function by keeping you vigilant and attentive to the possible dangers that surround the baby and the possible interferences that could get in your way as a caregiver. After all, these dangers are real, even if infrequent. A mother's acting on these "positive" fears does reduce accidents, miscues, and mistakes, and creates a better safety net for your baby.

There is even a question about whether they should be called fears. Yes, they feel like fears, but they are also responses to alarm signals that aren't noticed by non-mothers, to which only parents are sensitive. They could just as well be called "vigilant responses." In the course of evolution, animals, including human beings, have needed a heightened vigilance toward predators, heights, water, potentially dangerous strangers, bad food, sharp objects, and a host of other natural dangers. Today, there are few natural predators. Instead there is a new array of environmental dangers like high changing tables, cribs that are placed in rooms far away where the mother can't continuously monitor the baby, bathtubs, reactions to man-made products, and many others. These are the new predators that pose dangers to the baby. Mothers react to them exactly as if they were lions or wolves in the wild.

For too long, many mental health professionals have said that fears about a baby's suffocating, falling, or being dropped—in short, dying—are in large part expressions of a mother's negative feelings or unconscious desires to hurt or get rid of the baby. The notion that all intimate relationships contain a mixture of love and hate is accepted in most psychological theories. However, the interpretation of a mother's vigilant responses (fears) as a manifestation of ambivalence is a misapplication of theory that I find wrong-headed and destructive rather than helpful. It serves only to wound the mother and make her doubt herself at a profound level.

It is true that in a small minority of mothers these fears are too strong and vivid—no longer positive—and can cause great anxiety, especially when there is an impulse to act on them. We have all heard about mothers who can't manage to calm their screaming baby, and out of frustration and ambivalence shake them to shut them up, causing devastating physical damage, and even death. In such cases we are talking about women who need specialized, intensive help from qualified professionals.

In the vast majority of cases, however, vigilant responses and the feeling of fear that accompanies them are the mother's and baby's good friends, to be listened to for their constructive and protective function. Giving you a set of fearful thoughts is nature's way of assuring your baby's survival, and though the psychological strain will be heavy, the fear is actually your ally.

Hannah's mother expresses this heightened vigilance well:

> I've grown jumpy about things that never bothered me before. I never even noticed them before. It's as if I've grown a set of antennae that sense anything that might hurt my baby Hannah. I was reading last night in the living room (mostly napping, actually) and noticed the cat going upstairs where Hannah was sleeping. Even in my groggy state of mind I started thinking about the cat jumping in the crib and maybe suffocating the baby. Suddenly I was wide awake, up the stairs and pulling the cat out of her bedroom. Is that crazy or what? It doesn't really matter if it's crazy because I'd have done it anyway.

FATIGUE, THE TRIAL BY FIRE

As a new mother you will no doubt find that not only fear but also fatigue is your great enemy in the first weeks and months after the birth. It's important to understand about fatigue and what makes it accumulate and become so profound. First, remember that in the overwhelming majority of families you are the primary caregiver, shouldering the ultimate responsibility for your baby. This means that some part of you is always on the job either doing or delegating, or just passively preoccupied with baby matters, twenty-four hours a day. Vacations from the baby during the first year are partial at best and never simple, even when the baby is in good care. If you go out at night or away on vacation, the ritual of phoning home will help reduce your worry level, and mark your time away.

One of the reasons new mothers become so desperately fatigued is that very young babies are unpredictable. After one week home, it is hard to predict what a baby will be doing in the next fifteen minutes. After a few weeks or a month, it becomes easier to anticipate the events of an hour, but not always. It is only after many months that the eating, sleeping, and activity cycles become regular enough to let new mothers reasonably plan how to best alleviate their own fatigue.

The problem of fatigue is rarely resolved by going back to work. While many mothers experience work, even demanding work, as a partial relief from the constant level of caregiving pressure, the fatigue problem will not be surmounted. As one mother put it:

> I went back to work when my baby was three months old, but I was still up several times a night with her. Then she caught a cold and had even more trouble sleeping, interrupting my sleep more than ever. I was so tired, my face puffed out and I couldn't remember simple things like whether I'd brushed my teeth or not. After a few days of this, I moved into the living room with the baby so at least my husband could have a night's sleep. One evening I fell asleep at six o'clock, fully dressed, with my head hanging over the arm of the couch and the baby on my chest. I didn't even care. I would have given any amount of money in the world for a full night's sleep.

Another particular aspect of motherhood that makes it so fatiguing is that mothers are expected to be ready and able to act regardless of whether or not they know what to do. Even when they delegate a task to a family member or friend, the ultimate responsibility falls on them. What makes this so hard is that there is no way to be prepared for what might happen, and there is no job training that comes even close to anticipating exactly how situations will arise. This constant pressure takes its toll in fatigue.

As one mother described it:

> My child awoke every two hours for the first month straight. I was so exhausted that I really felt like I would go crazy if I couldn't sleep. My husband was back at work, and I was sleeping, feeding, sleeping, feeding all day and night. There was no longer day or night. All I could think of was that she would be awake in two hours so I better sleep when I could. One night around four in the morning my husband woke up and found me lying in the bed crying from sheer exhaustion.

All these elements lead to a chronic level of intense fatigue that most women rarely experience at any other time in their lives. You will find that this fatigue is inescapable. The fears for your baby's health and safety and your love keep driving you forward, making it impossible to quit or ignore her needs. Disoriented and weakened by fatigue, mothers at this stage often feel as if they are going crazy. This is the mother's trial by fire.

It is little wonder that the voices of experience tell you to sleep whenever you can. Take, borrow, or steal your sleep time from any activity that is not absolutely essential for you or the baby. The baby cannot thrive if you can't.

After the first several months, when the trial by fire is over and life takes on more regularity, most mothers look back on this early period as a blur—a seamless hodgepodge of pleasures and gratifications strung together with concerns, fears, and fatigue. You will be absolutely amazed that you got through it. As time passes and your baby continues to thrive week after week and month after month without any great problems (which is usually the case in spite of bumps along the road), you will become imbued with the unspoken knowledge that you have been tested by fire and validated, ultimately reassured about your fundamental maternal capabilities and abundance.

You emerge from the encounter with the first basic responsibilities of survival and growth knowing yourself to be an adequate and competent human mother. This hard-won self-knowledge is one of the cornerstones of your motherhood mindset. It adds an important layer to the motherhood identity, a layer that forms silently and progressively, but one that will prove an invaluable foundation for the mothering to come.

FIVE

Loving:
The Intimate Responsibility

ALONG WITH the concrete need to ensure your baby's survival, as a new mother you are faced with the equally awesome responsibility of developing an intimate, loving relationship with this new human being. Unlike the intimate relationships you have with parents, siblings, your lover, or your best friend, this one is unusual because it is based on interaction with someone who can't communicate in words. Ask yourself what your basic understanding has been of what it means to relate to someone else. For this new relationship, you will have to draw upon your lifelong understanding of intimacy. Unexpectedly intense, relating to your baby will call into action and into question all your talents for loving, sharing, relating, giving, and receiving.

As a new mother you will develop your own style of relating to and regulating your infant's experience. It is part of who you are, and your personal style will remain fairly consistent, whether you are playing with your baby, feeding her, talking to her, or setting limits. The power of this interaction lies in the fact that when you deal with your baby, you are simultaneously forced to confront important aspects of who you really are. You can experience this as either an opportunity or a disappointment, but there is no doubt that it will be revealing.

Before you became a mother, you probably took most aspects of your personality for granted. With the advent of motherhood, however, you have to reexamine a usually silent part of your personality—the way you form relationships—and you will be moved to ask many questions about the kind of person you are. There may be much for you to wonder about, to rethink, and possibly to change. Changing is generally easier if you allow yourself some time to reflect. In this case, you may find yourself thinking about what you are like in your relationships, and how that carries over to the way you want to be with your baby.

Some of the questions that arise in terms of how you love and attach to your new baby include: Are you capable of loving your baby, and, more important, *will* you love your baby? Will the baby love you? Will you be able to feel and accept his love? Will you recognize and believe that this baby is really yours, and will you believe that the baby has chosen you as his or her mother? Will you be capable of connecting with your baby adequately? And finally, as a mother, are you a natural? Do you have what it takes?

Psychologists say that at the heart of these questions is whether you can establish "adequate primary relatedness" with your infant. To understand this term, start with the word "adequate." This word acknowledges that there is no such thing as perfect mothering; rather, what most women offer will be "good enough" for their child's normal development. It may come as a relief to you to know that there is no such thing as the perfect mother, and that if you were perfect, it would be bad for your baby.

I say this because an essential part of every baby's education is the repeated frustrations, the ill-timed or maladroit maternal actions that force him to develop coping strategies, the missteps in the dance and false notes in the interactions that get repaired. Realizing that mistakes can be righted, and learning how to do so, is a fundamental lesson all of us needed to learn in order to live with others. Your baby needs to learn this as well. There are great advantages to making mistakes while learning to relate to your baby. The best we can hope for in parenting is that our mistakes are not too severe or left uncorrected for too long.

Continuing with the discussion of the term "adequate primary relatedness," we say "primary" because we're referring to a relationship between mother and child that happens before the child can speak. Furthermore, it is a relationship that involves the most basic elements of all intimacy: feeling attached, falling in love, taking an empathic stance toward the baby, establishing identification with him, and permitting the baby to become the subject of your reveries and preoccupations.

Where assuming the responsibility for your baby's physical survival tests your adequacy as a natural animal, this intimate responsibility for forming a loving bond with your baby tests your adequacy as a natural human being.

These two basic motherhood tasks—ensuring survival, and loving—work together. Loving your baby is an essential ingredient of making sure that you will work hard at keeping her alive. Conversely, your daily investments in the survival tasks provide interactions that forge an intimate relationship with your baby that cause you to love her more.

In this chapter, we'll look at three of the daily interactions of mother and baby that build intimacy and love between the two of you. They are activities you perform automatically and would not think to analyze as closely as I do here. However, the more closely you examine these activities, the more awesome they appear, and their importance to your baby's future becomes evident.

FEEDING

For about a year of your baby's life, mother and child carry on a basically nonverbal communication. Although you have never been formally taught this way of being with someone, you've never really forgotten it, either. This knowledge remains inside you, intact. You will learn to rely on it and call it "mother's intuition"—reading your baby's signals, sensing what needs to be done and when, and figuring out how. For example, let me describe a normal feeding which took place between one mother and her two-month-old son, Andy. Of course there really is no such thing as a "normal" feeding since each mother and baby create their own version which suits them. Nevertheless, most mother-infant pairs in our culture follow certain general steps in a feeding, depending on the baby's age. So this is an example, not an ideal.

When Andy first latched on to the breast and started to suck, his mother, Joan, without thinking about it, remained remarkably quiet and immobile. During this first phase of feeding, babies drink avidly and rapidly, taking in a lot of milk in the first minute or two with strong, businesslike sucking. During these first minutes, most mothers don't talk, or shift their position, or jiggle the breast or bottle—they do nothing that could disrupt the infant's intense work. That is exactly what Joan did—nothing—staying quiet, looking elsewhere, still able to see Andy in her peripheral vision so she could monitor visually any of his movements that she might not feel with her body.

Then, after a while, when the initial phase was coming to a close, Andy started to relax a little. His sucking eased up, his body became less tense, and he started to look around a bit. The edge was now off his hunger and he was ready to look, listen, and be touched while he continued to feed, but in a less urgent manner.

Joan intuitively picked up on this shift in his rhythm and intensity, changing her actions in response. In this second phase, she played a more active role in maintaining his intake of milk. Indeed, she had to, because when babies start to slack off in their sucking, or get too distracted by the world around them, or start to get "lazy" and even sleepy, mothers automatically have to jog their babies' nervous systems and recenter the baby on sucking. At this point, Joan, without thinking about it, jiggled the arm that was cradling Andy's head, kicking off a new burst of vigorous sucking.

She tried this two more times, without success. She then

resorted to a higher level of stimulation to recenter Andy on the job at hand, and jump-start his sucking. She looked at him and began talking to him. This started him up again, but only for a short while. She then moved to a higher level of stimulation, swinging her body from side to side and gently bouncing the arm that was cradling his head. That worked as long as she continued to do it, but after a while his sucking trailed off again. Convinced that he would and should take more milk, she upped the ante by rising from her chair, walking around, talking to him, and bouncing her arm at once. Again, he drank. All of this took many minutes.

The mother is like the conductor of an orchestra. (Or is it the baby who is the real conductor? Or does it shift back and forth?) She brings different instruments into play (jiggling, bouncing, talking) as needed to maintain the baby at the right level of arousal and activity so that the feeding continues at a reasonable clip. Like a composer, when the basic theme becomes less interesting, she plays it again with different instruments or at a different decibel level.

In the final phase of the feeding, Andy had almost finished and was sucking very lightly and intermittently. At this point, babies are somewhere between feeding a little more, sliding into sleep, wanting to play, or needing to burp. During this feeding, Joan had already burped him, and Andy was on the verge of falling asleep. Joan felt he could still take a bit more, so she switched into a much finer and gentler modulation of his alertness, using a level of stimulation that was neither so strong as to jolt him fully awake (and probably into a state of crying), nor so weak that it had no effect on him.

She took his left hand into her left hand (he was at her left breast), and began a very quiet, slow hand dance with Andy, a sort of pas de deux for the fingers. Without thinking, she provided enough constantly varying mild stimulation to keep the now drowsy baby feeding. And when he started to really slip into sleep, she stopped. Again she stayed quiet and immobile for a moment, as she had at the start of the feeding, while Andy sank fully into sleep. Only then did she pick him up and put him down to bed for a nap.

What we just described is a common enough event, simply one of many feedings during a day. Yet it is also a masterpiece of exquisitely orchestrated human interaction that takes place mostly beyond conscious awareness. It is important to say that not all feedings go so well. Many run into minor troubles such as overshooting or undershooting on the mother's part, delays, dead-ends requiring backing up, and temporary ruptures and repairs. The baby or mother may be too tired, moody, or preoccupied. Still, for the most part the basic moves are within the intuitive repertoires of both of them. The baby and the mother quickly learn the steps to this dance.

Feeding is a natural, vital interaction that can serve to give you confidence in your ability to relate to your baby. You will learn to read your infant's signals and you will develop the appropriate behaviors to carry out a mutually satisfying feeding. You will learn how you and your baby best fit together, and you will begin to think of your baby as a person in her own right. Your mother-child relationship will be established on the bedrock of simple interactions like feeding.

PLAY

A mother and child at play provide a different example of forming attachments because unlike feeding, playing has no practical goals. During playtime there is no milk to be drunk nor diaper to be changed. The only goal of play is mutual amusement. It is true that the best way to teach a young infant is by playing, but learning is not the goal of free play, only a wonderful by-product.

Because of this lack of a concrete goal, play is a most unusual activity. It is the easiest thing in the world to do, and at the same time one of the most difficult. Recall that at this age, the baby can't talk, can't yet manipulate objects, can't move around, and can't understand the words you say. This limits play to the sounds you make together, the facial expressions you exchange, the looking at and looking away, the movements and gestures and sharing of physical excitement. Play is limited to the very essentials of human interaction. It is a simple, pure, and unreflected activity—unencumbered improvisation.

To improvise well, you have to be sure of yourself, of what may come out, and of your ability to "play it" without any props. This is why free play challenges new mothers perhaps more than any other activity. It also raises familiar questions such as: Am I a natural? Can I be spontaneous? Can I adjust my behavior to my baby's behavior on the spot, without taking time to think? Can I strike the balance between initiating and following? Can I feel my baby's level of excitement and animation, and sense whether it is rising or falling, and fashion a behavior of the right dose (from some intuitive repertoire) to keep the play going? Can I lose my self-consciousness for moments so that I become fully preoccupied with my baby and slip into his skin or mind to know him better? To know him at all? To let him begin to know me? Is there enough of me to be known? Is who I am clear enough to be felt by a baby? Can we establish the most basic but simple human relatedness?

It is worth explaining at this point how free play works so that we can get to the heart of the issues that give rise to all these questions. Suppose that a mother and an alert four-month-old baby are face to face after a changing, or after the baby has woken up. They just look at each other for a moment, then the mother says, "Hi, honey," as a sort of greeting. The baby's face now brightens a little, so she says it again, "Hi, honey," probably with a slight change in inflection the second time.

This second time the baby breaks into a slight smile. What happens now? She can't say it again, or else the baby will start to get bored. Babies are very sensitive to repetitions and quickly tune them out. It is novelty that interests them most. So, without thinking about it, the mother intuitively varies what she says. Now she says, "Yeah, hi ya, honey." The baby's smile grows wider and his eyes brighten more. Then she says, "Yeah, you ARE my honey, aren't you?" In response, he throws his head up and backward and opens his smile wider. His animation is building even higher, perhaps more than she wants at this moment. So, the next time she says in a slightly quieter and low-pitched voice, to keep him from getting even more excited, "My little honey," changing the exact words to keep him still interested but at a lower level of excitation.

Of course the baby does not understand the words. For

him they are more like short musical phrases; at this age the music comes before the lyrics. The mother's words are sound objects. By varying each sound phrase, the mother engages the baby socially, modulating his level of animation and joy. She does this by creating a primitive theme and variation on the sound "honey." It is ideally suited to both keeping the baby fascinated and at the same time regulating his emotional state. All of this is done without much thinking. In fact, the mother is also keeping herself amused, which is most important—otherwise she can't play well. It is social improvisation of the most basic kind. This is the essence of free play!

Mothers know whether they do this well, whether it comes easily to them or not. They also know that these social improvisations don't work well if you don't love the baby enough to get lost in him or her for a while, or if you are too preoccupied with other life matters, or too inhibited for this kind of spontaneous activity, or too tired or depressed to be playful. All of these situations pose problems to the intimate responsibility of "being with" the baby.

Once again, nature usually steps in to protect the mother-baby couple from making a mess of this social choreography. The baby is robustly designed to be a virtuoso performer in his ability to regulate both the level of stimulation coming externally from his mother and internally from himself. He has an entire innate collection of behaviors such as looking away, shutting his eyes, averting his head, staring right through you at infinity, making recognizable facial expressions, vocalizing, stiffening or molding his body, flailing, crying, and falling asleep—which let you know if the level of stimulation needs to be shifted up or down.

On her side, the mother is intuitively a virtuoso performer in the moment-by-moment regulation of the interaction, based on the baby's signals. Together they evolve exquisitely intricate patterns of interaction, which at times appear to require much effort with constant repair and correction, and at other times look effortless. While things do sometimes go wrong, for the most part nature has seen to it that babies and mothers have evolved in tandem, with changes in one leading to complementary evolutionary changes in the other, so that they are designed to work "well enough" together.

Another example may illustrate some of the inner workings of intimacy found in most mothers. It concerns a game—in fact, one of the most popular of all internationally played baby games: "I'm gonna getcha." I have seen this game played in the United States, Western Europe, Scandinavia, Eastern Europe, and Russia. The words are different in each, but the vocal intonations and actions are the same the world over.

Here's how it goes. Six-month-old baby Rebecca is lying on her back. Her mother, Paula, introduces the main theme. She leans forward over Rebecca, walking her fingers up the baby's belly and chest toward the neck. As she starts the finger-walk she says, "I'm gonna getcha." (To "get you" is of course to tickle the baby's neck under the chin.) Immediately Rebecca becomes alert with pleasure.

Paula then repeats the theme two seconds later. Babies are very good at estimating short intervals of time. After the second time Rebecca knows that her mother's third finger-walk up the belly will occur in about two seconds. She is watching her mother's preparation for the next finger-walk.

This time, Paula introduces the first variation. She delays the finger-walk for half a second and elongates the phrase "I'mmm gonnnaaa getcha!" Rebecca's expectation stretches, and with it her level of suspense and excitation as well. Rebecca now expects the next finger-walk to occur two and a half seconds after the last one, so Paula introduces yet a further variation. She waits, holding back the fourth finger-walk another whole second, so Rebecca has to wait three and a half seconds before the mother says, " I'mmmmm goooonnnaaaaa getchhha!", with a voice yet higher pitched and more full of suspense than before.

Rebecca is now wriggling with delight and animated expectation. At this point, she figures her mother is going to increase the delay a little more each successive time—a game of increasing temporal violations. (One could ask how a baby could possibly do all that, but it is remarkably simple. It is basically no different from keeping or knowing the beat of music. At all ages we are extremely sensitive to any change in beat, which is what is going on here.)

So for the fifth finger-walk, Rebecca estimates that the walk will start around four seconds after the last, and she starts to get ready. It is then, before the baby is fully ready, that the mother introduces the last, the "punch line," variation. She suddenly launches her hand to Rebecca's neck only one second after the last time, well before Rebecca figured it would come. The game then ends with a neck tickle and Paula saying, "GOTCHA!!!"

This last variation violated the baby's expectation on the short end rather than the long end, as did the others. Rebecca, whose whole nervous system has been stretched to the maximum positive excitation, then explodes in laughter at being brought up short. And they both laugh together. The game, a play of temporal variations that regulates the baby's state, has been resolved, and a wonderful moment has been shared.

As you have undoubtedly found, these time-tested games (peek-a-boo is another) are a great aid to mothers. Not only do they work for all babies, but they give mothers something to fall back on when they are too tired to improvise, are uninspired, or are busy with another task. One mother explained her solution to calming a fussy baby in the car:

It's sort of embarrassing to confess what I do when I'm driving and the baby starts to fuss in the car. I don't think she's really unhappy; I think she's bored. However, there's not much I can do when I'm trying to get somewhere. She's belted into her car seat, and we've still got fifteen minutes to go. I've developed a whole routine for these situations, and one way or another I can usually get her attention and make her forget her woes.

First I hand her a cracker, but if food doesn't do it, I start talking. I tell her where we're going and why, in an animated voice, emphasizing certain words like her name, Meggan, and the name of her little friend Nikky.

If all fails, and she's still fussy, I start to sing. I call it the "See See" song. It has no particular tune, but lots of rhythm. "Who are we going to see, see, see? Meggan's best friend Nik, Nik-KY." On the "KY" sound, I kind of squeal a little bit, or tap the dashboard, clap my hand on the seat, or even honk the horn. Inevitably she starts to giggle, always anticipating that ending. Of course, I look completely foolish, and will probably have my driver's license revoked, but it stops the baby from crying.

These simple games and improvisations test you as a mother and add new pieces to the creation of your motherhood identity. Since you are responsible for regulating your baby's excitement and pleasure, you will learn how to guide without overcontrolling. You will learn to be sensitive enough to the baby's signals to determine whether the game is progressing too slowly or too quickly, or when it is time to begin a new one. You will learn when the baby's level of pleasurable excitation is too high and might spill over the edge and turn into crying.

The reason for going into such detail about the tasks involved in these intimate responsibilities is that over time you will realize what a privileged period of your life it is to have a baby. During these early years, not only are you creating your motherhood identity, but you also have the opportunity to rethink and reinvent yourself as a person. There are few opportunities for adults to do this, but becoming a mother is one—as is falling in love.

Psychologists refer to these major events in life as normal crises. A normal crisis forces a partial dismantling of your habitual way of being and demands that you put yourself back together, often along somewhat different lines. In this sense, early motherhood is potentially a "constructive crisis" offering a space and time when personal change is not only easier than usual, but even necessary. Early motherhood is a crucible of change where new identities are forged from old ones. The more you can see and reflect on what you are doing, thinking, and feeling during this period, the more you can influence the direction of these possibly far-reaching changes. With this in mind, we return to our exploration of the ordinary, daily activities between mother and baby.

All of the moment-by-moment choices or decisions you make in the course of a feeding or a bout of play are deep expressions of who you are as a person. What experiences do you tolerate well or poorly? Which do you prefer and seek out, and which do you want for your baby? Do you love excitement? Do you look for it? Is that a part of yourself that you value? Or do you prefer to construct your life more around a center of tranquillity from which you move outward? Who you are, who you like being, and who you want the baby to be will all be reflected in how you regulate your baby's experience in these simple repetitive activities.

In these apparently senseless games the baby adapts to the mother's range of acceptable excitement. What is at stake here is momentous. Your style with the baby directly reflects how much joy and hilarity and how much calm and quiet you expect and tolerate in being with someone else. You are being given an opportunity to modify your old expectations in order to create an environment conducive to your baby's healthy, happy development.

Your style of regulating the baby's experience will resurface when you begin to regulate your baby's exploration of her environment, once she begins to crawl and then walk. Before too long, your style will show up in how you teach your infant to speak. What will your strategies be for introducing new words, for tolerating mistakes, confusions, and frustrations? Your style of interacting will jump into the foreground again when it comes to setting limits (a subject of utmost interest to mothers of toddlers). Will you be strict, tolerant, permissive, or flexible? And even later, when your child starts to tell you what happened to her at school that day, how will you respond to your child's efforts? Will you work to find out what actually happened, or will you let her narrate her own elaboration of the event? Will you tolerate holes in the story, or contradictions, and if not, how will you repair them? Will you be more interested in the facts, or the telling?

In all of these details of life, the baby is getting basic lessons in what it is like to be with another person, what is to be expected, tolerated, and desired. These are lessons he or she will carry forward into future relationships.

You, laboring in the special workshop of mother-baby interactions—that crucible of change—are getting the rare chance to work and rework new ways of being with yourself and others.

IDENTIFYING AND LOVING

Another important part of primary relatedness is the ability to identify with your baby. To identify is to mentally slip into your baby's skin or mind by way of empathy, and then be able to alter your own feelings to conform to those you imagine the baby is having. The end result is that you feel as if you know what it feels like to be the baby (for a moment, anyway), and through this understanding, to get to know your baby better.

When you allow this empathic exchange, you establish a special emotional link to your child. You have put something of yourself into this little person, and she into you, marking the beginning of a unique relationship. It is important to note here that anyone can adequately provide the physical care for a baby, but very few people besides the parents or grandparents or other close relatives are in a position emotionally to accomplish the full work of identification that gives rise to love.

We have visited orphanages in places such as Romania where children have been placed at birth and live under the worst conditions. These infants' development is retarded, and they generally continue to have problems even after they have been adopted. The staff provide good enough physical care, but the lack of genuine emotional ties precludes the possibility of the sort of identification these babies need to develop emotionally.

Now and then in these orphanages, we have seen one or two infants who look much better than the twenty or so others in the same ward. It turns out these babies have become the favorite of one member of the staff, the person's "darling." The staff member will carry this baby around with her, and react to the baby differently than to the others. Favorites receive a sufficient dose of identification and loving so that their development course is far more favorable. Identification and its partner, loving, are crucial. A moderate dose ("just good enough") goes a long way.

Many observers of babies and mothers have commented on the capacity of mothers, under usual conditions, to identify with their babies. We all have the capacity to identify with others, but it seems to be especially heightened for a mother with her own infant. Many mothers say that they are relatively impervious to other women's babies, feeling no particular empathy, but that they form an immediate and intense connection with their own child.

Take this simple account of a lunchtime meeting with a new mother:

Before I had children of my own, I went to lunch with a good friend who had just had a baby. We were used to talking nonstop for an hour or so, leaping from subject to subject without interruption. This time everything was different. She had the baby in a little travel seat on the floor next to our table. I remember how startled and a little uncomfortable I was by her level of involvement with her newborn.

Throughout the meal my friend spent most of the time peering down at the baby, murmuring to her, running her finger over the baby's cheek, making faces at her, and responding to the baby's every movement. We got very little talking done, and I couldn't understand what she saw in the baby that was so interesting, so captivating. Not until I had my own baby, that is, then I understood entirely.

Some mothers wonder about their ability to identify with their baby. They wonder whether they will be able to establish a unique relationship with their child. This can lead to concerns about whether the baby would care, or even know, if another mother took over. Or it may lead to fantasies that her baby was switched at birth, and that the one at home is not really hers. These mothers question the bond between themselves and their baby, yet cannot figure out what is wrong. In more extreme cases, there actually is a problem that needs to be investigated. These are the exceptions, however, and most mothers simply have passing concerns about these issues. After all, this kind of immersion in another person has not happened to them in exactly this way ever before. It is part of the unknown terrain that mothers find themselves in.

To identify well and consistently with your baby, you must fall in love with this little being. Falling in love is the engine of interest and caring that powers the empathic act. Lovers enter easily into each other's minds, each ready to share his inner world of experience with the other. This is what "getting to know you" is all about. It's how the emotional ties of a relationship are forged. Falling in love with a baby is certainly different from an adult love affair, but the overwhelming passion is the same.

Engaging in the intimate responsibility of loving is crucial for the optimal development of your baby. It also adds another dimension to your motherhood mindset, and thus makes a big contribution to shaping your new identity. Of course, this process will not happen in a vacuum. You will likely turn to other mothers at times for guidance, support, and affirmation. We turn to this subject in Chapter 6.

SIX

Seeking Affirmation

As you struggle with ensuring your baby's survival and developing intimacy with this new being, you will start to reach out, finding in yourself an extraordinary need for exchanges with other women that will affirm your motherhood experiences. You must get the support you crave, both psychological and practical, in order to carry on as a new mother. The driving need and search for and the obtaining of affirmation from experienced mothers appears at first glance to be a simple matter, but as we shall see, it will lead to a path of self-discovery that is an essential component in the formation of your motherhood identity.

THE PSYCHOLOGICAL SUPPORT
OF OTHER WOMEN

The need for psychological support is felt immediately after the birth. We have interviewed many mothers about their hospital stay right after the baby's birth, and asked them how they looked for support and where they found it. Here is a typical answer that suggests what kind of psychological shoring up a woman looks for:

> My answer sort of surprises me. Each morning at about a quarter past seven, the cleaning woman came by to do the floors and to arrange my hospital room. She was about fifty and already a grandmother. First thing, she would always come over to my bed and say hello and look closely at the baby and at me. She usually said something like "Oh, your baby's looking so good," or "You're doing just fine together." Things like that. And we would talk for maybe five minutes. She told me about her grandchild or her experiences with her own children. We would just talk about mother-baby things. Then she went about her business. I grew to look forward to her visits every morning. They did a lot for my morale. Oh sure, the visits by the doctors and nurses were important and reassuring, but they were more medical or technical. My husband's presence was essential. Still, that cleaning woman was in some important way the high point of my day.

There are many variations of this story. They all point to the new mother's need for some kind of validation, encouragement, witnessing, and support, specifically from another woman who is more experienced in mothering than she.

Remember that motherhood is like a craft, and all beginning mothers need to apprentice with some kind of model or guide—a sort of master craftswoman—who has already been there. The role of the guide is not just to give advice and information. Much more, it is to surround you with a psychological environment in which you can feel secure and trustworthy, and encouraged to explore your parental capacities.

Let us call this special psychological environment an "affirming matrix." Some clinicians call it a "holding environment," almost as if the mother were being held in a sustaining embrace.

The affirming matrix often has at its center the wish for a benign mother figure or idealized grandmother who can perform the positive roles of a mother without the inevitable bad parts. This is a dream solution that is rarely realized. The new mother's mother may be too far away, or no longer living, or the relationship with her too problematic, but even so, most new mothers seek elements of it whenever they can. Mothers have a profound need, whether conscious or not, for psychological support that expresses itself in the urge to swap information and observe other mothers in action. Wherever mothers find each other, whether in the park or in play groups or at the pediatrician's office, an exchange of information and perception takes place on many levels. These interactions satisfy the need for assurance (I am taking care of my baby adequately), learning tricks of the trade (So that's how you keep the pacifier from getting lost), measuring how you are doing (I figured out how to quickly collapse the stroller to get on the bus), and belonging to the new domain of motherhood (I am not alone in this new land).

One experienced mother remembered vividly her visit with another new mother and her infant.

My husband and I went to visit friends who had a week-old baby. Both our children are older, so it was fun to see a newborn again. Our friends are somewhat isolated from their families because of geography, and Sarah, the new mother, latched on to me the minute I walked in the door.

Over our hour-long visit, Sarah never put down the baby, but many times brought him over to me with a question: "Do you know what this is, this gook in the corner of his eye?" "Doesn't he look alert?" "Why is his skin red there?" "How did you bathe your babies? I'm not sure about this thing we got to go into our tub." "It's hard to tell when he's sleepy, isn't it?"

I kept reassuring her, remembering how helpless I felt with my own first child. It was almost hard for me to see how desperately she wanted my approval and advice, and I don't know how much I actually helped. This was a woman who practically ran a law office, but at home with the baby she had no idea what to do. Her husband couldn't help much, either, because he knew less than she did.

Although your husband may provide critical emotional support, he cannot provide an affirming matrix simply because he does not have the legitimacy of experience that a proven primary caregiver has. Also, as we discussed earlier, with the birth of the baby the interest and concerns of most new mothers undergo a shift as they become more interested in women and less in men, more psychologically involved (consciously or not) with their mothers, and less with their fathers. This shift is already in place as you begin to explore possibilities for a new and workable affirming matrix.

Many new mothers turn to someone from their past for support—the most obvious candidate being their own mothers—but your affirming matrix doesn't have to center on her. It can focus on anyone who played an important role in providing your primary care—a grandfather, an older sister, an aunt, or all of them. It can even include your fantasy of what an ideal parent might be. One mother was surprised to discover that her role model wasn't in her own family, but rather from a family she knew as a young girl.

> When I think about myself as a three- or four-year-old, all I can remember is our neighbors, the DeVoes. The DeVoes had six children of their own, but they seemed like a happy family, and we spent a lot of time there. I used to sit in Mrs. DeVoe's kitchen after school, and she treated me like one of her own. There was always something for me to eat, and she cared what I had to say. No one at my house seemed to care. My mom worked, and didn't have the time to pay much attention to me.
>
> I don't know how Mrs. DeVoe did it. She had enough of her own kids to care about, but she always had time to hug me, and feed me, and listen to me. I'd like to be a mom like her.

Your ideal caretaker may be your mother, a friend, a relative, or a composite of several people. She may be living or dead, present or absent, but you can be sure that she will play a major role as you set your own mothering course.

THE REACH OF THE AFFIRMING MATRIX

In spite of so many changes in women's and men's roles in society, early motherhood remains the business of women to a surprising degree. It is important to recognize this fact whenever one attempts to untangle personal, political, and cultural influences we deal with on a daily basis.

In fact, new mothers have little trouble putting together an affirming matrix. It almost evolves on its own. In a research study we conducted several years ago in Boston, we asked new mothers whether they had contact with people after their baby was born, whether anyone came to stay with them, who visited, and whom they talked to by phone.

The surprising response was the huge amount of daily contact these new mothers had with women who were more experienced mothers. In the average day, each new mother had more than ten different contacts, in the form of either visits or telephone calls, almost one for every waking hour.

One of the very real benefits of this matrix is that it ensures that the new mother will rarely spend long stretches of time alone. It has long been suspected that mothers who find themselves socially isolated or unable to form a support matrix are at higher risk for having problems with the baby, and also for depression. For most new mothers, the biggest practical problem is to juggle visits and telephone calls so you can still tend to the baby and get some sleep. However, in finding the best balance for you, don't forget that the supporting contacts with other woman are not a social luxury but a psychological necessity.

Sometimes your own mother is the one who spends the most time with you in the beginning, whether she sleeps over to help with night feedings, just visits, or cooks and takes phone calls. If you are fortunate enough to have a willing mother around, she may become the centerpiece of your support matrix.

Of course some new mothers find that their own mother's visit comes at a price. As Lucy, a new mother, said, *Well, my mother wanted to come and stay for a week. That's about as long as I could take it. But she is a help with the house and shopping. I just hope that I can put up with all the negative stuff and not slip back into old ways with her.*

But despite the doubts and dangers, most new mothers have very positive relations with their own mothers during this time. In fact, some find that the relationship with their mother becomes more positive, more realistic, more mature, and in general takes a leap forward.

Next in importance after your own mother will be your mother-in-law, though the harmony of this relationship will depend very much on her relationship with her son. After her in importance will come sisters, aunts, and grandmothers from the mother's side of the family, providing they are experienced mothers themselves, and after them, experienced mothers from the father's side of the family. It is interesting that the matrix is made up not only of women, and experienced women, but most often women from the mother's family of origin. One stays close to home during this first phase of motherhood.

What about the men? Of course your father and father-in-law visit and talk on the telephone, but they are generally not the ones who initiate the contact. Your friends follow the same general pattern, with female friends tending to keep more in touch than male friends. Among your female friends, the ones that are already experienced mothers seem more likely to participate in the matrix. In fact, women tend to make numerous and lasting friendships that date from this time in their lives. Years later, many women will say, "This is my friend. We had our babies together."

Male friends will call or visit, but more often than not, after asking how the baby and mother are doing, they will slip back into the subjects that used to occupy their conversations prior to the birth, such as what's going on at the office. The role of the male friend seems to be to bring the outside world to the new mother, leaving the intimate details of babyhood to the domain of the female matrix.

MEMORIES OF CHILDHOOD:
THE SILENT CONTEMPLATION

As we have seen, beginning in pregnancy the mother-to-be starts to think more about the maternal figures of her early life. Women realize, often with a kind of surprise, that their own mothers went through some of the same things they are now experiencing. This may come as a new thought for them, and spark their curiosity about their past. This curiosity continues, often unconsciously, well after the baby is born, and may reveal itself in dreams and sudden memories. At other times, however, it is quite conscious, and involves straightforward questioning about how your mother was to you when you were a baby. Some mothers are acutely aware of the extent to which the past with their own mothers has come alive again. For others, this revisiting of the past is more subtle.

Why does all this reactivation of the past occur? Part of

it has to do with your search for models—your wondering what to feel about or do with a new baby. As with other new life situations, you automatically review your past experiences to find in them anything that might be useful for handling the present challenge.

The general idea of using the past as a guide to the present is supported by many of our new notions about how memory works. A traditional view of memory is that it is a sort of personal library in which each experience is stored like a book, and filed on a shelf by a code. It was assumed that the mind retrieves memories much as we access a card catalog, bringing up a faithful rendition of the entire original experience.

A more recent view suggests that there are very few whole original memories—no books, not even full paragraphs. Rather, experiences are stored in fragments of small memory traces, not one of which by itself makes much sense or composes a whole remembered experience, let alone an "original" memory. Thus, memory consists of a multitude of traces spread around the brain. When you remember something you select various traces and construct a whole memory from them. But the construction is never the same as the original experience. In fact, each time you remember something, slightly different traces might get chosen and assembled somewhat differently. No two memories of an original event are exactly the same.

What determines which traces you will pick out and what kind of assembly you will make of them? At the moment you remember something, you are in a particular situation in a particular state of mind and set of emotions. That context determines the meaning you will place on the memory and the details you will select to remember.

Let's say you are stuck on a hot day in a long line of cars going to the beach, and you suddenly think of a car your family had when you were very little, and how the seats would be too hot to touch when it sat in the sun. Perhaps you hadn't thought of that car in years. The moment when you have the thought is called the "present remembering context" and it not only determines which fragments will be chosen, but dictates how they will be assembled to make up a whole meaningful memory.

Each time you remember something, like the particular car of your youth, the memory experience is necessarily unique because the circumstances of the remembering context are never exactly the same. The next time you remember the car, you may be in your house watching television and the memory will be triggered by a commercial. The act of remembering is something we do in the present and not in the past. We remember in order to better understand what is happening now. In this sense, as odd as it sounds, we use the past to remember the present.

This view of memory can be applied to the new mother. When you are with your baby, you constantly find yourself in new "present remembering contexts." This happens when you embrace the baby against your chest and feel his soft head nestled against your neck, or when in the course of a changing, your baby is wiggling, screaming, and inconsolable. Each of these moments, and there are many every day, makes up for you a novel "present remembering context" that will pull up fragments from your memory and construct them into something meaningful that may help guide your present actions.

Since your baby is the present context for you, it is

inevitable that you will scan the traces of memories that are relevant to this situation. Logically, the memory traces you pull out of the file will concern your own experiences of being mothered. What else is there for you to fall back on, or use as a guide?

All of these considerations bring us to one of the most emotionally charged questions you will ask yourself: Will you be like your own mother?

"WILL I BE LIKE MY OWN MOTHER?"—PATTERNS OF ATTACHMENT

Many recent studies suggest that the pattern of attachment you establish with your baby is determined in large part by the pattern of attachment you and your mother had. This pattern of attachment refers to the way a mother and baby act toward and feel about one another when they negotiate the comings and goings of separations and reunions. An individual pattern has clearly emerged by the time the baby is about a year old and is starting to be mobile. Starting now, not only the mother but also the baby can initiate a departure and a return.

For a baby, separation from his or her primary caregiver is one of the more traumatic yet frequent aspects of normal life. It is especially difficult when the baby is under stress, is in a strange place, is feeling tired or sick, or is hurt, or if the separation has been long. The behaviors that best reveal an individual's pattern of attachment are what the mother and baby do when they come together after a separation. This behavior differs from culture to culture.

In our culture, at the moment of reunion after mother and baby have been separated, they run to each other as soon as they see each other. Babies usually reach out to their mother in a gesture that asks to be picked up. The mother either picks the baby up or kneels and enfolds him. Then they hug each other for a moment. The hug is a vitally important behavior. An embrace with both arms that presses chest to chest is probably the single most reassuring thing that human beings and also the great apes do with each other. Many babies nestle their head in their mother's neck, adding a little more to this special embrace.

After the hug has done its magic, the baby will be ready to leave and pull away. The mother may add a parting caress, or pat on the back, or ruffle of the hair. At this point, the baby has been psychologically reattached (some call it refueled), and can then separate again and go about the business of playing. This whole reunion scenario need only last several seconds to reconnect the two partners and repair the separation. This behavior is called the "secure" pattern.

There are two "insecure" patterns of attachment in our culture. In the first, the mother and baby seem to avoid one another at the reunion, almost as if the reunion were not happening and no one had returned or, for that matter, ever left. In this avoidant pattern, the baby appears to do nothing when the mother returns. There is no mutual approach and no hug. It is almost as if the baby is denying the importance of the event. Indeed, most of the mothers whose behavior can be characterized by this pattern would reject the baby or react negatively if he did seek a more demonstrative reunion. The baby has learned this, so by doing nothing toward the mother he is actually keeping her closer to him. These babies, despite appearing not to react to their mother's return, are, in fact, exquisitely aware of it and show many inner signs of anxiety.

The second "insecure" pattern is the opposite. The infant seems ambivalent, on the one hand showing signs of strongly seeking attachment and on the other refusing the mother's approach. The net result is that the reunion behaviors are exaggerated. It is more intense and takes longer. The mother is forced to be more demonstrative and must do more, almost as if the infant were using a strategy to get more attachment behavior out of the mother.

One of the reasons these patterns of attachment are so important is that they are among our best ways of predicting how the baby will adapt psychologically in the years to come. These patterns are fairly good predictors of how the child will be with peers as a toddler, and later with teachers and other children in preschool and grade school.

There are probably many other patterns between mother and infant beside the attachment pattern that tend to get passed on from one generation to the next, but the attachment pattern is the one that child psychologists have studied the most. What tends to happen is that you as a new mother will replicate with your own child the patterns of attachment you learned as a child. We call this the "intergenerational transfer" of a behavioral pattern.

We assume, and common experience suggests, that there are many other aspects of living that may be transferred to some extent from one generation to the next, such as ways of showing love, ways of disagreeing, fighting, and showing anger; ways of negotiating differences; levels of tolerance for different kinds of behavior; ways of sharing or not sharing one's emotions; ways of being curious and exploring the world; ways of reacting to change; ways of receiving new information and ideas; and ways of demonstrating the ties of loyalty and the traits of honesty.

The same influences that lead to intergenerational transfer can lead to a rejection of these behaviors in the next generation as well. It is often said that certain traits skip generations. For instance, if the grandparents were strict, the parents will be more permissive, and their children will, again, be strict when they become parents. Also, many of these intergenerational transfers are fairly specific to sex, the sons being raised like their fathers and the daughters like their mothers.

Intergenerational transfer retains, on the whole, the status of folk truth, but one that carries much emotional charge. When it comes to the specific area of mothers mothering as they were mothered, however, we have mounting evidence that intergenerational forces are hard at work, and powerfully influence the new mother as she begins to relate to her baby.

HOW MOTHERS ESCAPE
THE DESTINY OF THEIR OWN PAST

Fortunately, as a new mother you are not destined necessarily to repeat the old patterns of mothering you experienced. The more you can understand your relationship with your own mother and come to terms with it, the less likely you are to mindlessly repeat it. However, you must have a considerable capacity for self-reflection and insight in order to reach a mature and objective understanding of this relationship.

The relationship itself does not have to change as much as it needs to be understood differently. A woman who is able to reconstruct the story of her relationship with her mother with openness and perspective will have set herself free of the past, to a large extent.

One woman, Carol, provides a good example of this understanding.

> My mother was the worst mother in the Northern Hemisphere. She didn't want me in the first place. She was neglectful and when she got angry, she sometimes slapped me in the face. And then there was a long period when she wasn't available to me. It was like when she came home she didn't notice I was there. If I approached her she got irritable.

As a girl, Carol clearly had an impoverished relationship and an insecure pattern of attachment with her mother. One might expect that she would repeat some of these patterns with her baby. But Carol went on to say,

> It sounds pretty awful, but in fact there were good moments too. I think that it was very hard for my mother in those years when I was young. Her marriage was already shaky when she got pregnant. And just before I was born, my father went to prison and my mother was all alone without any family around. I know that she was completely overwhelmed and would withdraw or get angry and lose her temper. That's when she would hit me.

But there were calm moments too, and some happy times. She had a beautiful voice and would sing to me and we would dance. That's what I most looked forward to. When I was about two years old my father came home from prison and it was hell. My mother began to drink and got more depressed and unavailable. Sometimes she would try, and we would go somewhere alone for the afternoon and have good adventures. They were few and far between, but she never gave up on it. She always kept trying when she could afford to, but she's not a strong person. It was not easy for her to overcome things. It's still not. And I was pretty active and needed a lot of attention, anyway it felt that way. It would probably have been easier for her and me if I had been a less difficult and active kid. But that's who I was. And that's who she was. And in our way we both tried hard.

Carol has put an enormous amount of reflective energy into trying to understand what happened, and why her mother related to her in such a negative way. She comes up with a rounded, fairly well-balanced picture that permits her to break the intergenerational pattern. In fact, Carol went on to establish a secure pattern of attachment with her own daughter.

Just as there are patterns of attachment between baby and mother, there are also patterns of adult attachment between women and their own mothers. These are in many ways similar to those we described between mother and baby. Some women deny or dismiss the importance of their past, as well as their current relationship with their own mother. They tend not to think about it, and do not see it as playing any important role in how they will be with their own children. They tend to be less involved with their mothers in the present, and do not expect them to play an important role as grandmother.

This pattern is similar to the "insecure" avoidant pattern of attachment seen between mother and baby discussed earlier in the chapter when we described the different styles of experiencing motherhood. In the avoidant pattern mothers view from a distance their own experience of being mothered. One of the problems with this pattern of adult attachment is that if you keep a great emotional distance from your own experience as a child, it prevents you from doing the kind of self-reflective work that Carol was able to do. This will tend to make it more likely that family patterns will be repeated.

Another "insecure" pattern of attachment between adult women and their mothers consists of being so involved and enmeshed in each other's lives that it is not clear who is taking on the mother role and vice versa. One problem with this pattern, which we call the close-up view, is that it is hard for the daughter to achieve the much needed emotional distance to see the relationship from a clear perspective. Again, this pattern makes it hard to avoid repeating the past.

Clearly, the kind of mother you will be is not simply determined by what happened in the past. It also has a great deal to do with the work you have done on understanding that past. Understanding and reorganizing your past into a coherent autobiographical story may at times be more important than whether what actually happened historically was good or bad.

SHIFTING TRIANGLES

As we have seen, the mother-father-child triangle of your youth in which you were the child is supplanted at the birth of your own baby by a new triangle in which you are the mother. With the emergence of your own motherhood, a third triangle forms and takes the center of the emotional stage for a while. This is the triangle of mother-child-grandmother. In terms of daily events and schedules, the triangle of the new family (mother-father-baby) demands the most time, attention, and physical effort. It is the triangle that the outside world sees and identifies you with. Alongside it, however, under the surface, is the new triangle of mother-baby–mother's mother. Quite surprising to new mothers is the hold this triangle has on their inner psychological landscape. For you as a new mother, this triangle's demand for attention and psychological effort must be met so you can liberate yourself and proceed with all your new tasks. This triangle is little talked about in our psychological theories.

Outwardly and practically, the husband is the most important other person for you besides the baby during this period. However, under "good enough" conditions that relationship does not have to be reappraised. Major readjustments may be needed but your partnership with your husband is understood, and in a certain way, can be taken for granted. That is not the case with your own mother. There you must engage in a reevaluation of your past and present relationship, and often at a depth that you have never gone to before. That is why we say that the mother-baby–mother's mother triangle becomes the hidden work space for much of a new mother's psychological energy.

As the weeks and months of your new motherhood progress, you will most likely find yourself at the heart of an affirming matrix made up of family members and both old and new friends. These will all be women with some mothering experience who can help you, provide a sounding board, and generally confirm for you that you are doing a good job in your new role. Of all the people in your personal matrix, none will affect you with more emotional force than your own mother. For this reason, whether your relationship has been good or bad, it will require some of your time, attention, and perhaps most of all, reflection.

SEVEN

One Mother Speaks

IN THIS CHAPTER, one mother reveals the progression of her thoughts during the first year of her baby's life. Her concerns about new motherhood coupled with her particular personal history, her hopes and fears, and the culture of which she is a part all merge to form her new identity. With enormous candor she lets us know what her inner world is like as it flows underneath the ordinary acts and events of caregiving. This mother touches on all the main tasks that we have been discussing: survival, loving, and seeking affirmation. Her account is especially telling because she is quite normal and is, in fact, a good mother. While unique, hers is also an ordinary tale.

This forthright account may help you feel more comfortable with your own worries, fears, and hopes, similar to those that each new mother almost invariably feels. As you become more at ease with these preoccupations, it is easier to think openly about them, to share them, and thus to deal with them better.

When my son Nikolai was born after eighteen hours of excruciating back labor, the crown of his head banging against my tailbone with every contraction, the first thing the delivery nurse said was "I don't like his tone." The doctor, who did everything including hanging him upside down and slapping him on the back, couldn't get him to cry. "You didn't have Demerol, did you?" she asked, as she had only just arrived for the pushing. "He looks like a baby on Demerol." And, as if we weren't worried enough, he had an enormous black and blue bump on the side of his head. My husband, Michael, and I were afraid that our worst fear was being realized—our child was brain-damaged.

Our fears about Nikolai at his birth were, thankfully, unfounded. After my failed attempt at getting him to latch on—"You can try," the nurse had said, "but I don't think it's going to work"—Michael followed our drowsy baby down to the nursery, where he let out a forceful wail in protest against the bath, assuring us that he was okay. Our pediatrician, more to quell our fears than his own, ordered a cranial sonogram. "This is just in case he can't get his shirt over his head when he's three," he told us. Up in radiology, we were able to see, through the soft spot on our baby's head, his beautiful, perfectly formed brain.

"He's going to Harvard," the technician said. Michael and I both breathed a sigh of relief, but secretly I felt terrible guilt at what I saw as my rejection of him during those milliseconds after his birth that seemed to last for hours. I had pulled away from my newborn, in an effort to ready myself in case he were going to be taken from me, as if I could protect myself from this terrible love.

Now, as Nikolai's first birthday approaches, I see that both my fear that he was brain-damaged and the way I withdrew in reaction to that fear were part of what has become a familiar cycle in my life. It's a pattern of fear and withdrawal that manifests itself in my feeling that I won't be able to connect with my child and that, one way or another, I'll lose him.

Of course the pattern didn't start with Nikolai's birth or even with his conception. Not long after my parents separated, when I was eight, my mother gave me a book about divorce. There was a chapter called "The One-Eyed Monster," and I remember turning to it immediately, thinking that whoever wrote this book understood that ever since my parents' divorce I'd been afraid at night, and maybe they'd be able to tell me something that would comfort me, something I could use at midnight when I couldn't sleep and thought the squirrels I heard on the roof were really a murderer coming to take care of what was left of my family. But what the authors had meant was that a child of divorce is like a monster with only one eye (translate: one parent at home), afraid of losing that as well, and being left blind (translate: alone). In a more general way, the authors were exactly right—out of my parents' divorce a monster had been born in the form of loss. Not only did I lose my family as I knew it, but I lost my sense of competence and entitlement, my sense that I was both lovable and capable of love.

As commonplace and banal as it was in the late sixties,

my parents' divorce was a sudden death to me—a death of home, a death of happiness, a death of love. "Mommy and Daddy both love you very much," my mother told my brother and me, "but Daddy doesn't love Mommy anymore." With those words we both dissolved into tears because we knew about love, we knew that our house was built on it, that our lives depended on it and without it we couldn't survive.

Another chapter in the one-eyed monster book explained that my parents' divorce wasn't my fault. I never thought it was my fault. Whatever had killed my parents' love had done it quickly and silently, with no warning. So from this I learned an important lesson: if it could get them, it could get me too. No one is safe.

Twenty-six years later, that message is still embedded in me; that and the feeling that because it happened to me, because my family imploded when I was eight, I am somehow undeserving of a happy family; that now, as a mother, I am unworthy of this bounty. I don't think my parents' divorce was my fault, but I guess on some level I feel it was my fate.

When I was older the monster manifested itself in anxiety that I wouldn't get married, which turned into the worry that I wouldn't be able to get pregnant, which turned into the fear that I'd miscarry within the first trimester, which turned into the fear that my baby would be born with some horrible malady. Somewhere I felt that such perfect happiness, from finding my soulmate to cradling a baby so that her warm head fit in the curve of my neck would surely never be granted to me, a daughter of divorce, a child of family unhappiness.

When I was pregnant I wouldn't let myself imagine holding my baby—again, as if I could protect myself from the devastation I'd feel if something did go wrong. The only indulgence I'd allow myself was imagining dressing him or her in different hats: a little baseball cap, a Moroccan skull-cap, the little three-pointed knitted hat that was a gift from my office mates.

I wouldn't buy anything for the baby, either. I was due in early September, but when August rolled around Michael and I still hadn't gotten a single baby undershirt. The gifts that were sent to us, tiny white beaded moccasins, a Peter Rabbit rattle, a stuffed Noah's ark with miniature pairs of cows, zebras, lions, and alligators, I secreted away on a shelf in the linen closet, barely daring to look at them.

Maybe because I hadn't let myself imagine holding my baby, I was completely unprepared for the love I felt for Nikolai. As he lay on my chest, his head so small on my shoulder, my love for him took me by storm. Hand in hand with that terrible love came a sickening fear. I remember a writer friend of mine with fourteen novels behind her telling me that she didn't write a word until she had her babies, that before them, she was a virgin. "They take you for ransom," she said to me, and I didn't know what she meant until I felt him against my chest, his breath so determined, his brow so intent on sleep, his hands flinching because, the nurse said, he was afraid of falling.

When I got home from the hospital I barely left the house for a month. I blamed it on lack of sleep and the fact that I'd had an exhausting labor, but mostly, I think, it was because I was exhilarated by how much I loved him, and didn't want to burst the magical bubble that surrounded all of us in the apartment. At the same time I was devastated by that love and by the knowledge that I would never be safe again.

Another friend said, after I pressed her to tell me what it was like to have a baby, that for her it was very much like what open-heart surgery sounds like. Open-heart patients are often hit with a "third-day" depression that has been attributed to sleep deprivation. More than that, though, it's a reaction to "extracorporeal circulation," which means one's blood circulating outside the body. It can take heart patients months to recover from that experience. Mothers never do.

In those first tender days after we brought Nikolai home, it was painful to me when my in-laws held him. It was less the fear, albeit irrational, that they might drop him or otherwise harm him than the feeling that *I* wanted to be holding him, that he should be with *me*. I couldn't breathe easy again until he was back in my arms, where he belonged.

When I looked at our dog, our sweet, docile Rosie, who until the birth of Nikolai was our baby, I could see only a carnivore. I was terrified that some atavistic twinge would kick in and she'd steal Nikolai from his bassinet, snap his neck, and eat him for lunch.

When friends dropped by unannounced with their toddler, it was all I could do to be civil to them, as the child who had before looked like a sweet baby to me now was a huge unwieldy creature teeming with germs from day care. What were they doing bringing him into the same room with my pure, untainted, and vulnerable newborn? The first time Michael and I took our tentative steps outside with our baby, I was shocked at my reaction when people we knew from the dog park tried to peer into the stroller. "Keep away," I wanted to say.

Suddenly I saw and heard everything through the eyes of a mother. I couldn't bear any bad news, much less the news on television. One reported death meant the infinite pain of one mother, a plane crash meant that pain multiplied by infinity. I felt as if I had entered into the secret club of motherhood with its combined joys and terrors, but at the same time I noticed that no one was really talking about the terror.

"I wasn't prepared for how much I'd love him," I said, looking for communion at a meeting of new mothers, my first real outing, when Nikolai was a little more than a month old. We were going around the circle sharing what had taken us most by surprise. "I didn't think I could love anything more than I loved my dog," I added, trying to lighten it up a little, feeling self-conscious as my statement was met with an awkward silence. But what I'd really wanted to say was "Aren't you terrified? Aren't you afraid that something's going to happen to your baby? Or to your eight-year-old, or to your teenager or to your grown son? And then where would you be? How are we going to let them out of our sight? How can I leave him with a baby-sitter when she could turn away and let him fall out a window? How can I take him to day care when the building could explode? How can I let him take the school bus when it could slip off an icy embankment or be hit by a speeding train? How can I let him go to a party on a Saturday night when he could get into the car with a tipsy driver? How can I let him get on a plane to go to college when it could ignite in the sky or do a cartwheel on the runway?"

But the things these women in this new mothers group were sharing were more about the lack of sleep, or the difficulty of getting around the city with a stroller, or debating about whether or not to return to work.

Afterward, though, one of the moderators came up to me and said she'd been moved by what I'd said, and that in Anne Tyler's *Dinner at the Homesick Restaurant* there's a character who tries to lessen that feeling of terror and vulnerability by having another child, and instead she finds, of course, that the feeling has doubled. Finally, I had some acknowledgment that what I was going through was normal. Once you are a mother, there is no escape.

I dutifully signed up my husband and me for infant CPR, thinking that having the know-how to resuscitate my baby would impart a certain amount of confidence. It didn't. It was the first time we'd left six-week-old Nikolai with a baby-sitter. Being away from him for the first time and simultaneously having to contemplate the possibility of him lying lifeless and blue, his legs splayed open like those of the silver plastic infant facsimiles we were trying to resuscitate, was anything but reassuring. When the nurse told us stories about two friends of hers who had "lost" their babies, one because she'd done a blind sweep for food when her baby was choking, causing the obstruction to lodge itself farther down the baby's throat (never do a blind sweep) and one because the baby had strangled himself with a phone cord (never leave your baby alone with the phone), I felt sick to my stomach.

I know that every mother has her fears and every mother handles them in her own way. One of my friends speed-dials the pediatrician more often than she calls the Chinese take-out; a woman in my new mothers group obsessively compares the rolling over, crawling, walking, talking progress of her baby against the rest of ours, feeling that as long as hers is measuring up, everything is going to be all right. Another friend is obsessive about cleanliness, as if by protecting her baby from germs she can protect him from the vagaries of life. I come across as fairly relaxed in comparison to many of my friends. "Easygoing," and "laid-back" are two terms that have actually been used for me as a mother.

It was during a walk with Nikolai and Michael that I started feeling that my fear was intrusive, ruining my time with my family and interfering with my joy. A little boy who must have been eight or nine rode by on a red bicycle and Michael said to Nikolai in his stroller, "That'll be you, little guy," and instead of picturing the same thing Michael was picturing, Nikolai at eight speeding around the Riverside Park flowerbeds on his bright red birthday bicycle, I pictured instead how racked with grief my husband would be if this didn't come to pass, if his son didn't get to grow up.

I don't know if I worry more about losing my son than the average mother, but I know the toll it takes on me and can only imagine how it will affect Nikolai. I "check out" when I get afraid, whether it's a fear of, ironically, not feeling connected, fear of not being able to control his crying or manage his crawling, fear of illness, fear of random violence and natural disasters. The one thing my myriad fears have in common is that they compromise my sense of connection with my baby. They take me out of my little world with him and leave me hovering above, a fearful observer. Not only does this rob me of the present with my son, but it takes away something from him, as well—his right to an untainted, unadulterated vision of his future.

Now, the day before Nikolai's first birthday, I not only feel guilt about that morning in the delivery room when I hung back from Nikolai, suspended in limbo, as if I were deciding whether or not I was going to keep him. I feel guilt about all the times I've withdrawn from him. I find that being with my baby, really being present with him, is something that I have to actively give myself over to. It doesn't come naturally to me, and lately it's been especially difficult. He seems particularly demanding now, always crawling into something he shouldn't be, needing to be entertained in a way I'm not accustomed to. I find it exhausting and so I get into this "My turn, your turn" thing with Michael, the effort being lately to get away from Nikolai. Part of my need to escape comes, I know, from the expectation—my own expectation—that I must be totally present, that I must stimulate him constantly, and that I must enjoy it. I'm always trying to make up for what I fear I lack. My presence alone isn't enough: I have to be an über-mother.

When I was two and my brother was in preschool, my mother felt isolated and, I'm sure, a little bored. She wanted to pursue her studies, so she went to graduate school. One of my aunts told me that when my brother and I were little my mother would sit in a chair reading a book while we played on the floor by her feet, and she would glance down at us occasionally. At the time I heard this, and I think I interpreted it in the spirit in which it was meant, it sounded like neglect. Now, as a mother thirsty for any minute I can call my own, it sounds like the recipe for sanity. Still, I internalized the message that my mother was preoccupied and I have always been afraid that I inherited this trait and am not made of the stuff of my stay-at-home aunts, but of my more complex and conflicted mother.

"When you roll a ball to him, does he roll it back?" my pediatrician asked me at Nikolai's checkup last week, and I had to say I don't roll a ball to him. My cousin has taught her baby how to clap and how to throw away an acorn she's plucked up from the lawn rather than putting it in her mouth. Another cousin knows just where Nikolai is ticklish and makes him laugh a laugh I've never heard, never elicited. My friend says, "Give Mummy a kiss" to her nine-month-old and her baby happily obliges, leaning forward and putting my friend's nose in her mouth. The same friend hands my own son a toy, thus stopping his crying instantly, while I had been futilely bouncing his seat and saying, pleading, "Baby, baby . . ." All these things make me feel like I'm a bad mother, like I'm missing something other women were born with, some secret knowledge of how to *be* with a baby. Instead of simply rolling the ball, or asking for a kiss, or teaching my baby to clap, I worry that there is some magic mothering formula that I am not privy to.

I forget that Nikolai and I do have our games and routines and rituals, that we polka around the house, play peek-a-boo and the kissing monster, that I made up new words to "Twinkle, Twinkle, Little Star" just for him. I forget that when I'm nursing him to sleep, my hand holding his foot as he softly strokes my cheek, I am with him entirely.

So now when I find myself pulling back, afraid that my happy family will somehow be snatched from me, I remember Nikolai, so capable, so full of life, so generous in his love. He is the embodiment of life and connection, and I'm learning about them through him. If there's any formula for being a good mother, it's to let my child unfold, and to be there with him when he does.

Nikolai is standing on his own for the first time today. As I watch him and clap wildly, I am filled with that mixture of happiness and sadness peculiar to mothers. Almost a year into motherhood, I've come to revel in this strange concoction. Because as I clap, tears running down my face, I see that this clapping, these tears, are the weight and measure of my love.

EIGHT

The Diary of Joey and His Mother

LET US LOOK at motherhood in action, very minutely, as if under a microscope. So far we have presented mothers' narrations told after the fact and in broad brushstrokes. This story will present the experience of mothering as it is lived, from instant to instant, in the present. As a matter of fact, the interchange between baby and mother that I will describe covers about three minutes out of one hour in the almost nine thousand hours of a baby's first year.

I want to show from these three minutes how the moment-to-moment subjective experiences of the mother and the baby intertwine and influence one another. This mutual influence is played out in the small daily acts that make up our social life. To show this, I have continued with a story I developed in a book called *The Diary of a Baby*, an imaginary diary written by a baby named Joey. In a sense, it makes a companion book to this one because it describes the inner world of a baby as he is mothered, as this one describes the inner world of a mother as she is doing it. I have taken passages from the fifth chapter of the *Diary of a Baby* that describe Joey's experience of playing face to face with his mother when he is four and a half months old. To these, I now add his mother's experience of the same events, so that the interpenetration of the two worlds becomes apparent.

Before starting, I must explain how I arrived at a language for Joey so that he can tell his story in concert with the one his mother experiences. Imagine that none of the things you see, or touch, or hear have names. That is what it is like for Joey. He experiences objects and events mainly in terms of the feelings they evoke in him. He does not experience them as objects in and of themselves, nor does he experience what they do, nor how they are labeled. All his experiences consist of his action upon them and their effect on him.

Research suggests that when Joey's parents call him "honey," he doesn't know that honey is a word that refers to him. He doesn't even particularly notice it as a sound distinct from a touch or a light. But he attends carefully to how the sound flows over him. He feels it glide, smoothly and easily, caressing him; or he feels its friction, turbulent and stirring him up, making him more alert. Every experience is like that, having its own special feeling.

Joey gathers the swirl of what is happening around him into units that are dominated by feelings. The feelings are an amalgam of affect, thought, sensation, and perception. For this amalgam I use the term "think-feel"; I will say Joey "think-feels" such and such. What Joey goes through is probably no different from what we as adults go through, but we pay less attention to these basic units of experience. We are to a great extent distracted by the words and meanings we attach to events, so our sense of being is not focused on this basic level as Joey's is. We may best approximate Joey's experience when we listen to music, look at abstract art, watch or participate in a dance, or live through other quite special moments of being.

To give Joey a voice, I have had to borrow from sounds, images, weather, space, and movement—in short, from anything that might help capture the essence of his nonverbal experience.

I hope that this microview will help you think about your own mothering and how it works to express who you are and want to be.

It is nine-thirty in the morning. Joey is lying on his mother's lap, his head cupped in her hands, which are resting on her knees. He is facing her, ready to play. This is their usual time and position for playing together, face to face. Joey is Claire's first child.

Just before this moment, Claire hung up the phone after two calls, one from her sister and one to her mother. She is looking at Joey on her lap but not really seeing him. She is still thinking about her mother and sister. With one or two phone calls they can reinvolve her in family quarrels. Her sister, Nicole, is younger, beautiful, irresponsible, and difficult, running risks and getting into trouble, and then implicating and worrying her mother, who in a state of high crisis turns frantically to Claire to get advice and get calmed down. Traditionally Claire plays the moderator, calming the waters. Here she is again, doing just that.

While holding Joey face to face, looking at but not seeing him, she thinks:

> They do it every time. I can't be in my own life without being yanked out. Nicole should just stop, or at least shut up about what she's doing, and Mom should ignore her or stop overreacting. Okay, so she quit her job, is taking up with Jim again (the creep), and slammed her finger in the car door. It's not the end of everyone's world. This is the seventeenth act in the same play. Why doesn't Mom realize that, and why do I let her catastrophic reactions get to me and pull me in so I have to ease this new blow for her?

> What gets to me, too, is that I get used. The two of them are so busy being crazily involved driving one another nuts, that they don't even see me in the process. I'm not a real person in this, I'm a function—an intermediary, a "smoother-overer."

As she is thinking, her expression becomes flatter, and then sadder. She is facing Joey but staring through him, not moving. Normally they would have started playing, but not this morning. He searches her face. He think-feels:

> *I enter the world of her face. Her face and its features are the sky, the clouds, and the water. Her vitality and spirit are the air and the light. It is usually a riot of light and air at play. But this time when I enter, the world is still and dull. Neither the curving lines nor the rounded volumes are moving. Where is she? Where has she gone? I am scared. I feel*

that dullness creeping into me. I search around for a point of life to escape to.

Joey looks quickly at her different features. He knows them thoroughly by now. He knows their characteristic movements and what is supposed to happen. Her remaining expressionless, even for a moment, when face to face and gazing at him is unusual, although it happens now and again. It disturbs Joey that her face is *still and flat,* its features motionless. This flatness must be eerie to Joey, who is immersed in her face as his immediate and entire world of stimulation. He feels that she—*her vitality*—is absent, and wonders where it went.

After about three months, when babies know what to expect in a face-to-face encounter with their mother, they get disturbed if she deviates far from the usual. They are particularly perplexed if she suddenly stops interacting and her face becomes blank, or if they cannot rouse her to expression. In the well-known experiment called a "still-face procedure," a mother is asked to stop moving, to wipe all expression from her face, in the middle of an interaction, and just look the baby in the eyes. After about two and a half months of age, infants react strongly to this still face. They look about. Their smiles die away and they frown. They make repeated attempts to reignite the mother by smiling, gesturing, and soliciting her with their voice. If they don't succeed, they finally turn away, looking slightly unhappy and confused.

Joey's mother has unwittingly effected a partial and short-lived "still face" by wandering into her own thoughts. This distresses Joey for several reasons. Where he had expected to enter the magic sound and light world of a face alive and responsive (*the riot of light and air at play*), he finds stillness and dullness. Not only does he react to the lack of stimulation, but he may also be identifying with her. He may even imitate her and follow her into her sadness. Unable exactly to know her state, he can capture only the vague and confusing sense of her mentally hovering somewhere else that is unhappy. In identifying with her, he feels her *dullness creeping into me.*

Joey then searches her eyes, to find her. He has been looking all around her face, as babies often do, but now locks on to her eyes to find her soul.

I find it. All her life is concentrated into the softest and hardest points in the world, her eyes.

While Joey is searching her eyes, she is still mostly captured in the world evoked by the telephone calls. She thinks:

But it's always been like that. Even when we were little, Nicole knew how to get to Mom—how to involve her so the two of them were always locked up together. (Wait a minute, Joey.)

I never really found out what happened to Nicole's hand because of the car door, she was talking so fast. I imagine crushed fingers and blood all over the place.

It's like the time when we were kids. Mom was out and we were in the kitchen cutting something with a big knife and I cut my hand badly. Nicole tried to stop the bleeding and got blood all over her too. Just then, Mom came home and saw us. She automatically assumed that Nicole was the one who

was hurt and needed her, and not me. Without asking anything, she picked Nicole up in her arms and ran out of the
house to go to the hospital, leaving me alone, bleeding. Only
when she got to the car did she realize what had really happened. It was like I wasn't there—I don't get hurt—I don't
feel hurt. (I'll be right there, Joey, I'm coming).

This depresses me. And when I get down, the feeling that
comes over me is "not being there."

While she is thinking these thoughts, Joey watches her
eyes and think-feels:

*They draw me in deeper and deeper, into a distant world.
Adrift in this world, I am rocked side to side by the passing
turbulence underneath that ripples the surface of her eyes. I
stare into their depths. And there I feel running strong the
invisible currents of her vitality. They churn up from those
depths and tug at me. I call after them. I want them to surface, I want to see her face again, alive.*

Mutual gaze is a world within a world. Looking into eyes
that are looking back into yours is like no other experience
shared with another person. You seem to be able to feel and
follow the mental life of the other. At this moment Claire's
eyes are not sharply focused on Joey's, but they still vaguely
reflect her inner life. During this experience, Joey's shifts in
feeling follow, inexactly and impressionistically, the changes
in her subjective landscape. These changes are the *passing
turbulence that ripple the surface of her eyes* and make him feel
rocked side to side. Yet he needs more than to read the mirror
of her eyes. He needs her presence, the *invisible currents that*

tug at me. In this deep sounding of his mother, Joey is summoning her back to life. He *calls after* the *currents of her vitality* to make contact with them. What he most wants is for her to be there for him, but for that to happen her inner life must become directed toward him. Only then will she *be there.*

At this point, Joey tries to get her full attention and animate her. He widens his eyes, raises his eyebrows, smiles, and tilts his head backward with a funny sort of playful expression on his face. At this age babies are great experts in initiating interactions. His mother sees his movements and expression, and they start to pull her more fully into the present moment. She thinks:

> Oh, my Joey. I've left you alone, haven't I? Was I like you? So good and patient and not giving up trying to get them to focus on me? YOU ARE MY SWEETIE.
>
> (said out loud to him)
>
> You're like a skyhook pulling me up, my little love. You are my love. Yes you are. Aren't you?

While thinking and talking, she eases into a slight smile and moves her head forward toward him. She is progressively pulled into the immediate world with Joey. From among her many thoughts, she expresses You are my sweetie out loud to him with tenderness and appreciation. Joey quickly leans forward and returns her smile. They smile together, or rather trade smiles back and forth several times, while she says, again out loud, You are my love. Yes you are. Aren't you? synchronized with each smile.

While she thinks this, starting to smile and moving her

head toward him, Joey sees her face reanimated and think-feels:

> *Gradually life flows back into her face. The sea and sky are transformed. The surface now shimmers with light. New spaces open out. Arcs rise and float. Volumes and planes begin their slower dance. Her face becomes a light breeze that reaches across to touch me. It caresses me. I quicken. My sails fill with her. The dance within me is set free.*

As Claire becomes truly engaged with him, Joey experiences her face as sea and sky transformed. Specifically, he watches the movements of each facial feature as the smiles break over her face. After all, each feature for Joey is still also a form in space with its own architecture and movement. As the choreography of her smiles proceeds, her skin's tautness changes, and smile wrinkles appear: *The surface now shimmers with light*. Her cheeks widen and her mouth opens: *New spaces open out*. The curve of her cheek is raised and the corners of her lips pull up: *Arcs rise and float*. As the architecture of her face shifts, *volumes and planes begin their slower dance*.

Joey also experiences the entire transformation as a demonstration of the return of her life force, a return that affects him immediately. *Her face becomes a light breeze that reaches across to touch me. It caresses me.*

In reaching across to touch him, her smile exerts its natural evocative power and sets in motion its contagiousness. Her smile triggers a smile in him and breathes vitality into him. It makes him resonate with the animation she feels and shows. His joy rises. Her smile pulls it out of him. Then Joey fully releases it from within himself: *I quicken. My sails fill*

with her. The dance within me is set free. He is both responding and identifying now.

> *Now we play catch-and-chase. She blows on the patch of*
> *water around me. It dances with her breezes. I glide upon it,*
> *picking up speed, exhilarated. Passing outside the boundary*
> *of her wind patch, I coast on my own through flat, still*
> *waters. Still moving, but more and more slowly without her*
> *breeze, I call after her. She responds and comes after me. She*
> *touches down a fresh breeze just in front of where I now am.*
> *Riding her wind, I gain speed. I call her to follow me again*
> *and to lead me forward. We pull each other forward in*
> *jumps. We play leapfrog with the dance between us.*

Once a pair of smiles has passed between a mother and a
baby of this age, a process has already been set in motion.
What happens is this: Joey's smile and his mother's are
slightly out of phase with each other. This is as it should be,
since a smile takes time to grow on the face, to reach its
peak, and to fade. When his mother's smile is close to its
peak, it triggers Joey's smile. When Joey's smile hits its peak,
it reanimates her fading smile. By remaining out of phase,
they keep restarting the other and prolonging the duet, like
two kids having a contagious run of unstoppable laughter. It
is this passing in and out of her field of animation that
makes Joey feel as if he were moving into and then beyond
the local breeze she creates with her sequence of smiles.
Claire must feel the same way from her side. This is the
game of chase-and-catch they play. Each person's smile being
both cause and result of the other's smile, they end up
pulling each other forward in jumps. We play leapfrog with the
dance between us.

Then Claire starts a game, rather suddenly. She opens her face into an expression of exaggerated surprise, leans all the way forward, and touches her nose to his, smiling and making bubbling sounds all the while. Joey explodes with delight but closes his eyes when their noses touch. His mother then reels back, pauses to increase the suspense, and sweeps forward again to touch noses. Her face and voice are even more full of delight and pretend menace. This time Joey is both more tense and excited. His smile freezes. His expression moves back and forth between pleasure and fear.

Claire has thrown herself into the present moment of the game with an exaggerated flair, as if to shake off the cobwebs of the phone calls and memories. With each sweep forward she thinks something vague like, Yeah, here we are. With each reeling back, something like, Oh, there we are. It's as if she has finally liberated herself to be together with Joey.

Claire seems not to have noticed that Joey became tense and was at the edge of being overwhelmed at her last sweep forward to touch noses. So, after another suspenseful pause, she makes a third nose-to-nose approach at an even higher level of hilarity, and lets out a rousing "oooOH!" Joey's face tightens. He closes his eyes and turns his head to the side.

Claire now realizes she has gone too far, and stops her end of the interaction too.

Joey think-feels this:

Suddenly her wind shifts. The world of her face tilts up, spaces close, and she approaches me with a fresh, strong breeze. It flies at me on its own rising song and envelops me. In its embrace I slip forward quickly in effortless delight. She moves back, and her wind eases off for a moment—but only long enough to gather new strength. The gust sweeps toward me again. I await its approach, excitement growing within me. The wind hits me. I heel sharply to the side, yet also leap ahead, borne gloriously on a crest of joy. This second gust passes, her wind dropping momentarily again. I am moving at a thrilling speed, a little off balance. In the pause I try to right myself. But her next gust is rushing toward me, whipping up space and sound. It is upon me. I try to meet its force, to run with it, but it jolts me through and through. I quake. My body stalls. I hesitate. Then I veer off. I turn my back to her wind and coast into quiet water, all alone.

This third approach was too forceful and overstimulating. Joey is still *off balance from the second gust.* That is, his level of excitation is not yet under his control again. So when the third approach *strikes,* Joey can no longer handle the stimulation. It *jolts him through and through,* and he starts to fight it. Having passed beyond his tolerable zone of excitement, he falters on the brink of becoming overwhelmed, fearful and disorganized. It is then that he turns away and *coasts into quiet water, all alone.*

Claire stops the game abruptly. She is taken aback that it got derailed just when she was really getting into it. She is also shocked, in a way, to realize that she needed to throw herself into the game with so much force to undo or counteract the effect of her sister and mother. She senses something like this:

My God! I was acting for me, not really for Joey. I needed him—maybe even used him—to help myself, so I missed what was happening between us. It's just like what I said Mom and Nicole do to me.

She now waits.

Joey, no longer looking at her, recomposes himself. He senses:

This quiet place quells the turmoil inside me. It dies down and comes to a rest.

Joey is doing what we call self-regulating. He cuts out of his perception and then avoids the stimulation (from his mother) that was overwhelming him. He can look at something else far less exciting, or at nothing at all. There, his level of arousal will fall back into an acceptable range, his heart rate will slow down, and he will reenter a zone of lower excitation where he will again be open to external stimulation.

Claire sees this. In fact she is exquisitely sensitive to him when she is not preoccupied. While Joey is calming himself, she thinks:

My poor dear. You came to save me and I ended up pushing you away. I still wasn't all there for you. When I don't feel "seen" myself, I don't seem to "see" you well, either. I miss what you're telling me. But I'm here now. I know where you are, honey. I know that place, too. I will wait for you, just like you did for me.

After a short while, Claire senses that Joey is showing tentative signs of being ready to reengage with her, but at a very low level of stimulation. She then whispers to him. He turns his head to face her again. She breaks into a slow, warm smile, lightly touched with sadness. Joey experiences her invitation in this way:

After a while in the stillness, a faint zephyr brushes the side of my head. It refreshes me. I turn and see it gently ripple the water under a softer sky.

They reengage, quietly glad to be back together. Claire thinks:

It's okay now—it's okay—we're there.

The point of looking at this moment closely is not to make you worry: "My God, knowing that all of that is going on every second would drive me crazy. It would make me feel responsible for every little act, for breathing, almost!" That is true, but no one is supposed to even try to be conscious of all that. If you were, you couldn't act at all. The daily small acts exist mostly outside consciousness, where they belong. They are a part of intuitive parenting.

What happened in this moment was not bad or good. It was simply an interaction that was natural to the two people who Claire and Joey are, and to the unique psychological influences that play on their everyday life.

From one point of view it could be said that Claire made many insensitive errors, but I don't see it that way. She is doing the best she can at being a mother and being herself, and since she is the only Claire in the world, no one can be a better, more authentic Claire. Joey is learning how to be, and act, and feel in the presence of his mother—with the one person who will be the most important teacher of what it is like to be with someone. So Joey, too, is doing the best he can.

What will happen is that Joey's personality development will be shaped by the unique fit they make together. Let us look at Claire's tendency to be preoccupied, to get captured in the past and mildly depressed. What are the possible results of that on Joey's development?

He will learn several different ways of being with his mother. How he does this is fascinating. Infants are very good at picking up what makes something characteristic and identifying its essence. Each time an event is repeated, they try to identify the elements of the event that were there the last time it happened. These are called "invariant elements" because they never vary, are always there.

For instance, let us imagine how a baby could form a stable image of his mother's face, which is changing all the time. Suppose that early in the morning, he is hungry and cries to be fed. Mother gets out of bed and comes into his room. Her eyes are full of sleep, her hair is down, her face expressionless. That is face number one. She then leaves the room to get his bottle, and on the way throws some water on her face and puts her hair up and her glasses on, and goes in to feed him with a more pleasant expression. That is face number two.

Later in the morning she prepares to go out; she puts on lipstick, redoes her hair differently, and puts on a hat. She comes in to play with him for a minute, smiling most of the time. That is face number three. The baby has seen three different faces but does not believe that he has three different mothers. Instead, he identifies those features of her face that do not change, those invariant elements, such as the shape and color of her eyes, and the length of her nose relative to her forehead. He tosses out, so to speak, the variant elements: the glasses, hairstyle, lipstick, and facial expression. By pulling together the invariant elements, he creates a prototype of her face that becomes his "official" representation of what she looks like.

If we apply this same process of forming physical prototypes to something more interesting, like the typical interactions between mother and baby, we end up with prototypes of "ways of being with" someone. For these prototypes, the invariant elements are: what does it feel like to be with the person? What actions are performed and what inactions? What facial expressions are seen, what sounds are made? Given the characteristic ways that Claire and Joey are with each other, what are the various "ways of being with" her that he may come to rely on as predictable parts of his world?

One such way is for Joey to become a "reanimator," a charmer, or a life giver. Indeed, Joey is already good at that, and an important part of his relationship with his mother is his ability to pull her back into the present moment. We could speculate that as he gets older he will get even more adept at animating people and saving them from sliding down emotionally. He may even choose girlfriends and a wife who need these qualities in their partner.

Another "way of being with" for Joey and his mother involves his learning to seek stimulation elsewhere when she is too preoccupied to provide it at an appropriate level. He may develop a vigorous curiosity and learn to explore the surroundings on his own, even when he is in her presence, or on her lap. This special characteristic of this curiosity and exploratory bent is that it occurs with his mother in the background. His independent exploration is a solo activity but is experienced against a background figure. Accordingly, Joey may never be completely alone mentally, even when he is alone physically.

Joey will also have to learn to be a good self-regulator of his own states of overexcitation. These will occur at moments when his mother is temporarily insensitive, or forcing an engrossing engagement with him to pull her out of herself. He will become a good self-soother.

Finally, Joey will get to know a "way of being with" his mother that is like being in a mild depression, a "microdepression." At those moments when Claire tunes out, slows down, and is far away in reflections tinged with sadness, Joey will partially imitate and resonate with her inner state. He will become "acquainted with grief," and have something tender at his center, which is another way of saying he will have "soul."

Is all that so bad? Not at all, at least not in my mind. Because of the way Claire is, Joey may develop a certain charm, curiosity, independence, capacity for self-regulation, and soul.

If Claire were preoccupied, depressed, or insensitive most of the time, we would not be talking about Joey's acquiring traits that have both advantages and disadvantages. Instead we would be worrying about more serious problems that fall outside the range of "good enough" mothering.

All mothers want to be better mothers, even when they are already "good enough." There are many techniques, secrets, and bits of knowledge that can help you do better. Most mothers avidly acquire these useful techniques of mothering, which permit them to change themselves from the outside in.

You can also become a better mother by changing from the inside out. That is the main goal of presenting this micro, instant-by-instant description. It makes clear how thoroughly the way you act as a mother is an authentic expression of who you are, though not the only one. This recognition is important because it shifts your questioning from looking at the external information to a deeper reflection about who you are with your child, and how that expresses who you are as a person shaping who your child will become. Looked at that way, it becomes easier to use the motherhood experience to effect a real change in yourself from the inside out.

PART III

A Mother Adapts

NINE

Special Needs: Premature or Handicapped Babies

A S A WOMAN adapts to motherhood, she not only takes into account who her baby is, but also who she has become because of having a baby and who she wants to be in the future. This chapter focuses on the special problems of adapting to motherhood when a baby is either premature or has special needs.

Excellent information is available today concerning children with handicaps, and there are associations and foundations that can provide support for families dealing with this difficult situation. I would like to approach the subject of dealing with a child who has special needs from a slightly different standpoint—the particular obstacles facing a woman who is trying to develop her motherhood identity, and discovers that her infant has either a delayed development or a severe handicap. Of all the obstacles that confront a new mother, learning that her child is not completely healthy can be the most staggering.

THE END OF THE FUTURE

Remember the importance of imagination for a new mother—how you work and rework your future on the landscape of your mind in order to adapt to the dramatic changes in your life? Your imaginary baby, your dreams of how you will be as a mother, and your ideas of what your future family will be like all preoccupy your thoughts during pregnancy. It is vital that you play with the future in your mind as you try out different scenarios that will enable you to accept the new life you will be living.

It is a rare woman who doesn't wonder what it would be like if something were wrong with her baby. You probably thought about this when you were pregnant, and wondered whether you would have the strength to give such a baby what he or she needs. Yet even if you fully imagined the negative possibilities during your pregnancy, and even if there were realistic evidence that your baby could have a physical problem, you can hardly predict the shock of the actual arrival of a handicapped child. For any parent in this situation, there is a tremendous amount of psychological work to be done in the weeks and months that follow the birth.

With the news of a baby's problem, you can no longer clearly imagine this baby as a preschooler, an adolescent, an adult, as a parent, or as someone who could take care of you when you grow old. You've lost not only your ideal baby but, more important, the freedom to anticipate the future of your baby and family.

As one mother said, *I always imagined that one day I would be walking with my two children, holding each one by the hand. Now there is a gaping void in front of me. I don't know if I will have to spend my life taking care of an infant who could never walk. I don't know what will become of me.*

The birth of a severely developmentally delayed or handicapped baby is a trauma that virtually stops time in its tracks, and when time stops for you, your ability to imagine beyond the present halts as well. Suddenly your future is unpredictable, and emotionally unimaginable. At the same moment, your past, full of the hopes and fantasies of pregnancy, is obliterated and becomes too painful to remember. Parents are held prisoner in an enduring present.

Imaginings about the future of your child aren't like photographs—a thin slice of time. They are more like a moving time line of wishes, fears, and fantasies in the form of little stories that unfold toward a future. When you as a mother get caught in the present without an imaginable future and with an effaced past, you're deprived of the full range of the imagining process. You can't elaborate stories about your baby or your motherhood, and are thus cut off from the mental work space for planning and creativity. All of this goes on inside you, while in the physical realm you're scrambling to accept and manage a situation that calls upon all your capacities for love, patience, and resiliency.

For a mother, the process of coming to grips with a handicapped or delayed child follows a predictable path, though the specifics are anything but predictable. Some characteristics common to these mothers are the necessity of seeing past the handicap, doubts about their own competency as mothers, handling the challenges to loving, identifying with and attaching to the baby, and finally the essential need to reinvent the marriage along new lines. Invariably, the situation begins with learning about the possibility of the handicap.

LEARNING ABOUT THE BABY'S PROBLEM

Each child with a handicap has his own unique history. In the same way, each family has its own course of discovering the nature and consequences of the illness. The agonizing and indeterminate nature of the discovery process often causes as much trouble as the baby's problem itself.

For the family, the discovery usually starts the moment the medical staff informs them, or in many cases delays informing them, of a problem. Everyone knows the usual rituals surrounding a birth, with words like: "Congratulations, Mr. and Mrs. Jones, you have a healthy baby girl!" Any significant deviation from these words sends out an alarm signal that registers deep in the parents' consciousness. This first moment is a key time for the parents, who often feel as if a time bomb has been dropped in their midst.

Sometimes the full nature of the problem isn't clear, and the staff simply announces that the baby is "at risk." Even though the medical personnel may have handled the news with great care and sensitivity, they often act as if their job is done once the family has been informed, leaving in their wake what is essentially a handicapped family. Although the staff cannot say more than they actually know or can reasonably predict, the family understandably feels isolated and bewildered by countless questions.

The truth is that in most cases no one, including the medical experts, knows how the situation will turn out, or according to what timetable. This uncertainty is the most difficult part of the parenting experience, the part that engenders an insupportable anguish as well as a paralysis coming from the inability to imagine the future. Parents usually look forward to each of their baby's developmental milestones, like sitting up, walking, or the first words, almost as they would anticipate passing a test. When these milestones aren't reached at the expected age, it can activate waves of anguish, sadness, or guilt.

Uncertainty in these situations may stretch on for years. Baby John's story illustrates an all-too-familiar scenario. At birth John seemed perfectly normal. When he was two months old, his first-time parents started to really worry about his sight because his face didn't light up when they held an object in front of him. They consulted their pediatrician, who agreed that the child needed to see a pediatric ophthalmologist. Several weeks later it was determined that the boy was partially blind, and the doctor recommended a battery of tests.

When John was four months old, his parents were told that he probably had a degenerative disease for which there was no cure, and that he would be completely and irreversibly blind before his first birthday. Devastated, the parents sought another opinion. The second ophthalmologist agreed in general, but was less certain of the bleakness of the diagnosis and the timing. This rekindled the parents' hope, and they sought more opinions. Not until John was eight months old did they get a medical consensus: John was totally blind.

One might think that the diagnosis would bring an end to the long period of discovery and uncertainty, but that wasn't so. John's parents never gave up hope, becoming avid readers of all the literature they could find on their son's illness. When John was thirteen months old, they read about a new treatment being tried in London. They made contact with the people and went for a consultation, but John was not thought to be a good candidate for treatment.

As John approached the age of two, his parents read about a new operation being performed in Madrid. They brought him there at age two and a half for extended consultations, but again, they did not get the go-ahead for the operation.

At my last contact with the family, John was four years old. The parents had made other attempts to reach out for medical help, but were beginning to lose hope. They had not given up entirely, however, which in their case prevented them from completing their mourning for John's loss of sight. They had started to imagine John as a young man who was blind, an important psychological step toward acceptance, but were still unable to let go of the hope for his healing. This got in the way of their being able to formulate much-needed early strategies for his special education, such as having him learn Braille, because planning for special education to them signified the irreversibility of his condition. As the months went by, they lost valuable developmental time.

Although this may sound like an extreme case of prolonged uncertainty, it is not unusual. Acceptance of circumstances other than normal takes a very long time. One has to work through stages of denial, and try over and over again to cover the distance between the ideal imagined baby and the real, imperfect one. The situation requires walking a fine line of constructive realism. This line runs between pessimism on the one hand with its dangers of paralysis and despair, and optimistic denial on the other which prevents you from taking realistic therapeutic steps and establishing a more stable inner peace. This dilemma occurs to some extent for all parents when they compare their real baby to the one of their hopes and dreams; for parents of a child with any degree of illness, this dilemma is greatly multiplied.

In our culture, premature birth has become more and more common and deserves its own discussion. With premature birth the parents deal with all the issues that confront parents of any child, along with some issues facing parents of handicapped children.

The story of Nell provides a good illustration. Nell was born one and a half months early. The doctors alerted her parents to the possibility of some delay in her development, but accurately reported that it would be hard to tell how much of a delay for the first several months. The parents were left with their worry.

By the third month, Nell's parents began to suspect that all was not as it should be, and grew more convinced after seeing other babies of the same age. By the time Nell was four months old, her parents consulted the pediatrician, who agreed that Nell was somewhat delayed, but counseled the parents to wait another few months to see what would happen because premature babies frequently catch up.

When Nell turned six months old, the delay seemed to persist, and the family took her for neurological and developmental evaluations which lasted for several weeks. When she was almost eight months old, the medical staff confirmed that Nell was moderately delayed, but could make no specific diagnosis. They told the parents to play with and stimulate Nell so she would catch up to the normal developmental curve faster. The parents began to do this, and fortunately got some professional help in the form of physical therapy and special education.

This new regime in the household subtly but importantly altered the nature of the relationship between Nell and her parents. Her parents had become teachers as well as parents, now constantly stimulating Nell and devising new ways to promote, scaffold, and elaborate her learning. It grew harder and harder to just have fun and behave spontaneously. If you remember from an earlier chapter the importance of improvisation to a baby's development, you can imagine that Nell's parents found it almost impossible to improvise because they were working so hard at teaching and stimulating.

Nell's parents continued with their regime, and waited for results. They had Nell evaluated again six months later, when she was fourteen months old. Yes, the doctors said, perhaps she had caught up some, but more time was needed to tell whether the improvement would continue, and at what rate. In general, if these premature babies are going to catch up fairly fast, they usually do so by two years. In slower cases it can take up to six years, or perhaps in special cases, they may not ever catch up completely.

Often the premature baby will be four or five years old or started school (which is the ultimate test) before the parents have a fairly solid picture of the child's mental, scholastic, and social future. This was the case with Nell. By the time she was six years old and well assimilated in school, it was apparent that she had caught up. She was a delightful, intelligent, popular little girl. This story ended well, but until her parents were assured of her progress, they could not realistically imagine a future for Nell and simply become her parents. This is the excruciating reality of the discovery process, sometimes with a happy ending, but many more times with endless uncertainty.

A mother who endures this long and agonizing discovery experience also evolves an inner landscape significantly different from that of other mothers. All of the challenges that face any new mother confront these mothers as well, only with more intensity and less certain outcomes. Identifying the challenges for these women is far easier than prescribing the solutions, but I've endeavored to touch on both, starting with the challenges.

SEEING PAST THE HANDICAP

Most mothers look forward impatiently and excitedly to discovering who their baby will be; what will be her particular expressions, her character, and her approach to life. Worries about a handicap, however, and what and how much the baby will be able to do, often block any discovery of the baby's true personality. In the words of one distraught mother, *I can't see past her handicap. I can't see her!*

Recall that one of your vital roles as a parent is to be the one who sees as clearly as possible who your child is. What are his or her assets, talents, preferences, and natural inclinations and dislikes? Ideally, in identifying these you will help your child follow a path closest to her inner design. When the presence of a handicap blocks the discovery process, parents have trouble finding clues to the path that is right for their child. In a sense, the baby loses part of her individuality in their eyes.

IDENTIFYING WITH YOUR BABY

Inevitably, you see your son or daughter as a continuation of yourself, as someone with whom you can identify. Furthermore, the process of identifying with the baby is expected to be gratifying. Normally, you as a parent are pulled by empathy inside your baby's experience. A handicap may prevent this from happening, especially if the announcement of the handicap occurs before you are given the chance to bond with your baby. In such cases, your first reaction to your own baby as a continuation of you may be one of massive rejection. As one mother said to me, *I wish he would go back. This is not my baby.*

Not all mothers have such difficulty, but there are certainly women who find themselves barely able to tolerate being associated with a baby who isn't normal. Somehow the wounds to their self-image mixed with the sadness for the baby are too great. I have heard many times sad reflections such as this mother's: *I avoid going to the park when other mothers will be there. I can't take any remarks about Johnny, even the polite ones about how he holds his head, or his passivity in the stroller.*

Another mother spoke with sorrow and deep self-recrimination: *My daughter is like a dirty clown. I'm ashamed to go out with her.*

In spite of these obstacles to identification, most all mothers of handicapped children forge an attachment with their babies, even if the identification is slightly different from other mothers'. They are forced to see the world through their baby's eyes, to put themselves into his skin, and to live at the rhythm of life imposed by his handicap. This pulls different parts of the mother into the identification process than if the baby were completely normal. As one couple explained, *In the beginning, right after she left for summer camp, how alone we felt! It takes a while to put yourself back into the skin of somebody normal. It's as if we also were living with her handicap.*

HOW THE MOTHER SEES HERSELF

With the birth of a healthy baby, most mothers experience themselves as competent human animals, that is to say, someone capable of continuing the species by producing an intact baby. The mother of a handicapped baby is wounded at the very center of this task. She and the father generally feel a pain and a guilt that will color their parenting experience for the immediate future, and sometimes much longer. They may be haunted by the search for a reason for the handicap. As one mother described it, *I kept looking for what I may have done, or not done, for this to have happened. Somehow, somewhere, somebody must be responsible.* An equally anguished mother remembered, *I felt myself banished by God. How could a baby like that come from me? Am I evil?*

OBSTACLES TO ATTACHMENT

If a baby is premature, he may stay in an isolette in the intensive care unit for weeks or months. During this time you cannot play a major role, and sometimes no role at all in keeping your baby alive and thriving. Machines and the medical staff do that for you. Even your visiting may be curtailed so that opportunities to get to know your baby are limited. You will probably feel less special to your baby than the nurses, and most of all feel less competent. In short, you are prevented from attaching to your baby.

In an earlier chapter I talked about the patterns of attachment between mother and child, and how your relationship with your baby will probably be patterned after your relationship with your own mother unless you take steps to change it. I would like to add a little more about attachment here, which in the last few decades has become an increasingly important area of study.

Attachment refers to the establishment of a special bond one to another. This bond between mother and child is initially physical, keeping the mother near the baby, and when the baby can move about, it keeps the baby near the mother, or at least wanting to come back to the mother after his forays into the world. This attachment assures the baby's safety from the external dangers of the world.

The attachment bond, however, is also psychological, giving rise to a sense of security when the baby and mother are close together. The highest point of feeling secure, where one experiences a safe haven, is when the mother and child are in an embrace, chest to chest. A baby held in that way faces the world without fear.

It is important to remember that the attachment bond is a two-way street. The mother's attachment to her baby is faster forming, usually well under way during the first few weeks of the baby's life. It is fascinating to watch a mother's attachment come into being. Under normal conditions, right after the birth when the baby is cleaned up, the nurse or doctor brings the baby back to the mother and places it on the bed beside her. This is when the mother begins what I can only describe as a slow dance with her baby.

The dance begins when the new mother starts touching the baby's feet or hands with the tips of her fingers, gently, almost gingerly. At this point the baby is still a familiar stranger. As the baby accepts the mother's touch, and she gets to know his feet or hands, she slowly moves up the leg or arm. As she does, she touches with more assurance, using all of her fingers, not just the tips. She moves from the periphery to the center, toward the baby's belly and chest. As she gets there, her hand opens and caresses the baby's body with her palm. She may stay there a while, then, invariably, move up to the baby's head and cradle it in her palm, and perhaps lightly touch his face with the fingertips of her other hand, or her lips.

This process, varying from mother to mother, is her way of making this familiar stranger more familiar and less strange. She makes this baby her baby. She is forging the bonds of her attachment.

Many premature babies are in a closed isolette where

they can only be reached through portholes, and then only when gloves are worn. Inevitably, there are tubes running in and out of the baby, and often various machines nearby, and the noise of artificial respiration. Under these conditions the mother cannot perform her attachment moves. In addition, most parents are terrified of hurting this delicately balanced creature. They are torn between attraction, fear, sometimes revulsion, and always impotence. This situation can go on for weeks, during which the mother can feel a vast emptiness.

Recently new procedures have helped mothers overcome this particular attachment problem. Many premature units now use the "kangaroo method" in which the baby is medically cared for in the intensive-care unit while on the mother's chest, affording skin and body contact in spite of the tubes and machinery. This permits the mother and father to proceed with the attachment process. Not so incidentally, this method has proved to be better for the babies medically, who tend to gain weight faster than when in isolation. It also instills some sense of competence in the mother, although this won't be completely fulfilled until she is at home alone with her baby for a period of time.

OBSTACLES TO LOVING

The reality of the hospital setting and of the baby's condition can also get in the way of loving, which is not the same thing as being attached. Recall that one of the essential tasks of the motherhood mindset is to experience yourself as a competent human mother who is able to love the baby freely and fully and to be loved in return. This too can be threatened. Many mothers doubt whether they will be able to love this imperfect baby who has thrown them into a state of such chaos. Often she goes so far as to question if she really wants to keep the baby alive.

One mother of a premature baby hardly had any contact with her son for the six weeks he was in the hospital. She recounted how she went alone to the hospital to pick up her baby, whom she didn't really know at that point, or really even want. She put the baby in the infant's seat in the backseat of the car, but didn't secure him correctly.

When the mother pulled onto the highway, she found herself behind a swerving car, and had to suddenly jam on her brakes. This jolted the baby, and with alarm, she realized the infant had fallen out of his chair and rolled under the front seat. Immediately she pulled to the side of the road and ran around to the back door to gather up her baby. When she took him into her arms, it was the first time that she felt this was her baby and that she would take care of him. It was at that moment that she began to learn to love him.

As I mentioned before, the mother of a premature baby is not allowed the last weeks of pregnancy to prepare to meet her real baby. The real baby arrives when she is still highly involved with the baby of her dreams and wishes. This can further hinder her ability to start loving the baby immediately, as can a certain loss of self-esteem at not having completed the pregnancy, not to mention the stress that arises from the sudden and early birth. All of these conditions conspire to hinder the mother from being able to freely and easily love her newborn child. In most cases, however, the motherhood mindset soon comes to the fore, overshadowing the challenges to love.

REINVENTING THE MARRIAGE

In some cases, the mother of a handicapped child may think of the handicap as her own personal failure, not her husband's. After all, she might say to herself, it is up to her to produce and deliver a whole infant. She may feel especially responsible if the handicap results from some event during the birth process. Feeling already responsible, and anticipating her husband's devastation when he learns of the problem, she may try to protect her mate from the reality of the situation. One mother remembered that when it came time to bring their baby home, she wanted to go alone to the hospital to protect her husband from the anguish of the experience.

Parents try to protect each other in many ways, while the baby is in the hospital and for a long time afterward. It isn't uncommon for the basic care for a handicapped baby to fall more heavily on one parent, usually the mother, than would have been the case ordinarily. Many kinds of scenarios may evolve, but in most cases the course of the family's life will be permanently altered.

For instance, the father of a handicapped boy could be narcissistically wounded by the presence of the handicap to the point that it is painful for him to spend time with the son. The wife then protects everyone by taking over much of the father's role, in addition to her own. On the other hand, the father could make a powerful identification with his son, and take over much more of the caregiving than he would ever have done under completely normal conditions. In this case, he may become a better father than he ever would have been had his son not had a handicap. In any case, in a family dealing with a handicapped child, roles and alliances often develop differently than they would have after a normal birth.

BLAMING THE PARTNER

Too often it happens that one parent is considered to be at blame when the baby has a problem. This feeling could actually have a basis in reality, such as when one side of the family carries a particular gene, or when a certain physical or behavioral trait is known to run in one of the families of origin.

Blaming cannot take root, however, unless it falls on fertile ground—if one partner already mistrusts or dislikes a particular trait in the other, for instance. In such a case, the trait in question can become a fault line in the marriage into which the handicapped infant falls. The blaming becomes a continuation or exaggeration of a problem that already existed before the baby was born.

THREAT TO THE MARRIAGE

The arrival of a handicapped baby can pose new dangers to the integrity of any marriage, even a strong one. One mother explained, *We don't dare make love anymore. There just isn't any pleasure thinking about where all this trouble came from to begin with. Bad memories and associations come up, and make it not work at all.*

Other parents may find themselves isolated because their usual peer network suddenly disappears or is diminished. A child who is not like other children can make for parents who are not like other parents. They have no one to share their experiences and difficulties with and are often afraid of boring others, or fear that others won't be able to understand what their daily life is like. They find themselves socially isolated, which reinforces their sense of failure. *We had no support for a problem that overwhelmed us completely. We were thrown together, and that's all we had. There we were, alone, together, alone, alone, alone, and no way out.*

For these parents it's not just sex and social contacts that they lose, but many other props that normally bolster a marriage. They find themselves needing to spend a huge amount of extra time and effort in caregiving and, often, a huge amount of money for expenses they never anticipated. Their larger family may also keep its distance, making it even harder to find substitute caregiving for a night out, or for a few hours' break. Just taking a vacation can require enormous strategic maneuvers that other families don't face.

OVERCOMING THE OBSTACLES

Many couples faced with the problems of having a handicapped child pull together in ways they never thought they could, and emerge with a strong, loving, intact family which is more robust than it might have been had their child been completely normal. Many others, however, experience some or all of the obstacles that I have mentioned here, and all would agree that the obstacles are many and difficult, if not insurmountable.

Perhaps the most important way to approach the challenges is to explore what you are experiencing and find a way to share it. This is true for all new mothers and fathers, but especially so when there is a problem with the baby. The most rewarding sharing often takes place with other parents in similar situations, and with professionals who have a familiarity with the unique circumstances involved. Exploring, talking, and sharing are essential to identify one's fantasies, fears, and unfulfilled hopes, and to give shape to these experiences. Once they are verbalized, it is easier to examine them and then move ahead with life. Sharing also breaks through the isolation, real or imagined, that many parents feel.

It has become my conviction that the great majority of mothers with a handicapped or premature baby experience a form of trauma during the weeks and months after the birth. These mothers should not be left to fend for themselves without help—I am not thinking primarily of psychiatric help. A mother in this situation is not a psychiatric case, but overwhelmingly a normal person under the stress of extreme circumstances.

It's my opinion that what the mother most needs is a kind of professional accompaniment from someone with whom she can establish an alliance, and who will understand her experiences. She needs to be validated as a mother in those areas, small though they may be, where she can really feel like one. This companion should aid her in making contact with her baby, and teach her to better know the baby by showing her what the infant *can* do, and see and hear, and not only what he can't. Finally this person should be able to integrate all the diverse opinions and plans that inevitably come from the pediatrician, neurologist, ophthalmologist, nurses, physiotherapists, special educators, and others in the large team of professionals who will attend to the baby. These multiple opinions can fragment the mother's world if there is no one designated to coordinate and discuss it with her.

I would like to mention another way to deal with these obstacles, and that is to have another baby. I know the objections to this idea, bit I still feel that it should be seriously considered. One might think that before having another child, it is important to fully pass through the mourning period that accompanies the birth of a handicapped infant. However, this mourning period can take years, and perhaps deplete your time for attempting another pregnancy. Contrary to what you might think, the birth or adoption of a second child can often unlock the enduring present of which we spoke earlier.

A second baby helps the mother recover her sense of herself as competent. This reparation often permits parents to restart the flow of time, to envision once again a future for their family and themselves. The issue here is not one of replacing the damaged baby with a new one, but rather of letting the next baby help the first one and the family. A second baby also serves the invaluable function of putting the problems of the first into perspective, thereby relieving the first baby of unproductive scrutiny. The parents can begin to see the handicapped child better for who he is as an individual human being.

The problems in this area can seem enormous. However, parents who can explore their experiences, share them with others, and seek psychological counseling for the initial period of crisis and adaptation may progressively be able to clarify their situation and move away from the pain of it. This clarification will permit the parents to tame their circumstances and finally rejoin the current of time. They can learn to grow and love their baby in ways that they cannot possibly imagine at the beginning of their journey.

TEN

Your Career—When?

RECALL THAT YOUR motherhood mindset will not remain on the center stage of your mind forever. Very gradually it gets pushed to the background, where it remains intact, ready to be called into the foreground as frequently as needed. As this mindset moves into the background several months or years after the baby's birth, depending upon your circumstances, it must learn to exist in harmony with your other identities.

This is what the adaptation phase of motherhood is all about; bringing your many identities into balance with your life as a mother. Your other identities may include your role in your larger family, your role as a wife, or your position in the community, but perhaps the hardest place of all to find harmony is the bridge between the two roles of mother and career. Each mother's solutions to the inevitable conflict between work and baby responsibilities are crucial to her successful integration of the new motherhood identity into the rest of her life.

It would be a rare mother today who is not anguished, depressed, guilty, perplexed, or deeply ambivalent about the question of going back to work. Should a new mother work? If so, when should she return to the workplace? How important is it to spend the early years at home with your baby? When your child grows up, will you look back and wish you had arranged things differently? There are no fixed answers, and there are certainly no perfect, permanent solutions. There are only relatively good or bad compromises. Furthermore, each time you arrive at a solution, you should be prepared for it to change before too long because of unexpected events or unanticipated feelings.

POLITICAL AND FINANCIAL REALITIES

It is impossible to discuss the issue of mothers going back to work without taking into account the political and financial culture in which we live. So often the deeply troubling decisions you face appear to be unique to your family, and intensely personal dilemmas. In reality, the choices you have to make may be determined by society's political priorities. The vise that you can find yourself in may not be simply "motherhood" but may in fact be motherhood in the United States of America at the beginning of the twenty-first century.

In the United States, it is not uncommon for a pregnant

woman in the workforce to get either no maternity leave, or a scant three or four weeks. Some employers may allow more, but many times this is taken from a mother's personal time, sick time, or vacation time, or she receives no pay for the months she stays home. To add to the pressure, her job may not be there when she returns, or she may find herself subtly punished for staying home by a job that has moved on without her, absorbed by other employees.

In most European countries, women automatically get three to six months maternity leave, with an extra month allowed for nursing mothers. In Sweden, women automatically get twelve months off at 85 percent pay (until recently it was 100 percent). Even more striking, the new mother can use those twelve months however she wants over a period of seven years. She can take the whole first year off, take off half-time for two years, or take off three months a year for four years, and so on. The Swedish government has recently introduced a change to encourage fathers to take a greater role in the young family by requiring that the father take one of the allotted months to stay home, or the couple will forfeit their twelfth month.

Equally interesting, Swedish law is clear on the point that when the woman returns to work, she is entitled to enter the system at the same level of seniority or priority that she had before she went on leave. Under such conditions, Swedish mothers and fathers think very differently than their American counterparts about the importance placed on being home with the baby, at least in the beginning, as well as about the feasibility of doing so. In short, in America, our policies and work culture are largely responsible for a certain portion of the anguish and uncertainty that most mothers are forced to undergo.

I feel that in America, mothers are placed in an impossible and false position. The society may support, or give lip service to, strengthening the family, but at the same time makes it economically difficult for parents to balance work and family life. This results in countless families where the parents feel torn, unnatural, or inadequate in the amount of time they spend with their children. The whole issue of when to return to the workplace exists in a context that is stacked against the mother before she even gives birth to her baby.

Mothers today are all too familiar with the difficulties of balancing work and family, but they often overlook the fact that the compromises they are forced to live with are truly not their fault, but rather the consequences of social mores. In addition to the difficulties of scheduling child care, transportation, and time off from work when your family needs attention, many mothers carry the extra burden of guilt about the decisions they've made. For many mothers who are forced by family finances to return to work when their babies are young, this situation is a constant source of anguish and tension. Only a change of attitude in our culture, accompanied by a change in public policy, will help relieve this tension. It is shameful that our political and economic system does not support the optimal development of the child and family.

Although a father's active participation in the parenting process can give the mother a greater range of options, it only partially resolves the basic problems, and it often creates new ones. If the father opts to be the primary caregiver, the problems that plague mothers will befall him instead. Sharing the parenting is a workable compromise for some, but it is rarely a fully satisfactory solution.

The touchy question of whether a parent belongs at home full time with the baby is an individual matter. There seems to be a consensus that if the mother strongly prefers to be back at work, it is probably better for all, the baby included, if she does return as long as adequate alternative care is arranged. The majority of women, however, may want to return to work at some point, but not as quickly as our current policies force them to return.

On the basis of my experience and that of many others in the child development field, I think the optimal time for a mother to return to work full time is when her baby becomes two years old. At this point most babies have attached to their mothers, and have learned to trust this relationship. They have experienced a number of separations and learned how to tolerate them. Additionally, nature often lends itself to a two-year gap between children, because breast-feeding tends to inhibit ovulation. If the mother breast-feeds for a year or so, as in many societies, the second child will be born when the older one is about two years old and can walk and allow his mother to focus her attention elsewhere. Although optimal, this time frame may be difficult or impossible to achieve because of the family's financial needs.

THE CONFLICT BEGINS

Mothers start dealing with the issue of returning to work when they first become pregnant and start to envision their future. Women recognize early on the limited options available to them, and begin immediately to imagine different scenarios concerning staying home, leaving their baby with a family member, or finding local day care. Typically, few women can really predict how strong their feelings will be once the baby is born, or imagine just how difficult it can be to carry out whatever decision seemed feasible during their pregnancy.

Following are the thoughts of three different mothers whom you've met earlier in the book, and the strategies they devise during their seventh month of pregnancy for handling their work life after the baby is born. Margaret, an architect, is the most ambivalent. She finds herself pulled equally by the desire to stay home with her baby, and the pressure to stay with her job.

When I walked into the conference room for my annual review, all the partners managed to seem relaxed, but I knew there was an issue hanging like a sword over my head. We've got a huge contract coming up, and they want to know if I'm going to abandon them for this baby.

From the day they hired me, no one can say that I've let my personal life interfere with work. I've always told these guys that if I had a baby I would work until the day of delivery, and be back soon after. Jim totally understands the way I feel. We've decided to hire a caregiver who will be with the baby full time. The decision has been made—anyway I thought it had been, until recently. I'm not so sure anymore. I've actually considered what it would be like to stay home with a baby. And sometimes it feels good. I make up compromises in my mind. The other night I was picturing sitting at my drawing board with the baby lying on a blanket at my feet. What would these guys think of having a baby in the office? I can't picture going into a client meeting with a baby on my hip. Or, maybe they would let me work at home a few days a week, or cut back my hours? Not likely. As much as they like me and say they care about my personal life, they would replace me in a minute.

So I had a knot in my stomach in the conference room. Nothing was really changed there except for me. They were pushing a plate of pastries around, drinking coffee, talking the way people do who share a commitment. Finally my turn came up, and they all turned toward me,

"Well, Margaret, can we count on you for the upcoming project?"

"Yes," I said. "No problem. I'll be here one hundred percent. I will do everything I can so that you can count on me."

Was I lying? Yes and no. I was upset that I had to lie, and confused that I didn't really know, and mad that the whole choice I was being given was all wrong. Somehow wrong. I couldn't see the future very clearly.

Other mothers know already that they either want to or have to go back to work very quickly, and have come to accept the idea. The idea does not come, however, without a psychological price. Diana, a financial analyst, knew even before getting pregnant that her career would continue in spite of the baby. Her greatest concern is whether she will be any good as a mother.

I've stopped telling my secretary the plans for this baby because she looks at me as if I'm an alien. She has never heard of a new mother who hires a baby nurse. Well, let me be the first. I've already looked into the service, and they will send me a woman to be at the house from eight in the morning until supper time for the first three months. Best of all, she's trained to care for infants. What a relief. I know I sound hard. I'm being honest.

I expect to be back in the office within a month or so, as soon as things at home are settled. Carl will be a big help because he works for himself and can be around. It's probably a good thing for all concerned that I'll be at work.

Carl wonders if I'm secretly a member of some royal family. I would be comfortable having my baby cared for by a nanny and brought to me only when it's bathed, fed, and not crying. Of course I don't want the baby to love the nanny more than me, and I want to be involved in its life. Maybe I'll even find parts of myself I don't expect, and get caught up in it all right away. But I think I'm going to be a better mother when the child is older, when it can talk to me. That's when I'll take time off from work.

All this makes me feel sort of unnatural, as if I am supposed to be someone I am not, as if there is something wrong with the way I am.

The third mother, Emily, had already left her chosen career in the theater to take a more stable job when she found out she was pregnant. Emily tilts toward staying home with her baby and away from her career. There is a certain relief for her in not having to pursue her career for a while, although she too pays a kind of psychological price for her decision.

The women in my office are really friends. Everyone has advice, or a baby gift, or a story to tell. Nancy says that after the baby I can come back to work whenever I want, or for whatever hours I want. The funny thing is, I'm not sure I want to come back at all except to visit with the baby.

What I picture is having this baby with me wherever I am. I can imagine using those baby seats in the carts at the grocery store, going to town with a stroller, or wearing a front sack and having little arms and legs dangling out of it. That's what I want. I'm going to say good-bye to work for a while.

Having a baby is going to put to rest that other question too. So many people remember my romance with the local theater. I know I was good at it, but wasn't ready to do what it really takes to be a committed actress. People keep bugging me about it, though. And it used to be a question in my mind (I guess it still is), something like a failure of courage or ambition or something. But you can't pursue acting when you're having a baby. Things are resolving themselves, I think . . . I hope, and it feels natural, as if I was meant to go this path. We'll see.

Three different women, three different stories, and three different solutions to the mother/career dilemma. No one of the three is better or worse than the others. They are equally honest and realistic reflections of who that woman is and how she will confront the problem while remaining faithful to her own perceived needs and abilities. Most important, you must figure out what will make you happiest and most fulfilled, and strive to achieve that situation. Try hard not to let others tell you what you should do or feel. If you know yourself and what you can live with, you will find the best compromises for your set of circumstances. In the long run, the best solutions for you are very likely going to be the best solutions for the baby as well.

THE HEARTACHE OF THE DECISION

When, usually for financial reasons, a new mother must go back to work before she really wants to, she may experience a great sense of loss. Because the decision has been externally imposed, the new mother may feel emotionally wounded and may suffer from extended postpartum depression. Even worse, when the mother knows she faces a return to work after just three weeks or three months of motherhood she starts her grieving long before it is time to leave. This interferes with her ability to be with her baby even when she is still at home on maternity leave. She cannot avoid thinking of the pain that is to come.

Mothers who may have the financial ability to stop their careers and stay at home longer experience a different set of problems. They often feel as if they have dropped out of society and are wasting their education or their career opportunities. They have to fight not to feel devalued by certain of their colleagues, friends, and even family members. It's often very hard to handle the demands of a new baby and weather the judgments of the outside world, particularly when you have mixed feelings about your decision to begin with. Many women have worked quite hard to reach a certain professional level, and as clear as they may be about staying home, there is usually a streak of doubt or longing concerning their work.

Clearly, we as a society are doing something wrong if there is such turmoil, no matter what decision a new mother makes. We financially reward mothers who return to work. To support this we have gone on to produce an entire class of child-care workers. However, we can't afford to pay the caregivers too much because it would deplete the mothers' salaries and not make it financially worth their while to work. In turn we expect perfection from the caregivers, but not so much perfection that they threaten the maternal bond between mother and child. Everyone involved is put in an impossible position.

Today we see many mothers in the former East Germany who are experiencing regret about how they spent their early motherhood years. In the formerly communist part of Germany, most mothers returned to work quickly after their babies were born—a separation sanctioned by the culture. After the reunification of Germany, these women were exposed to the more flexible West German system, where a six-month maternity leave is the rule. In an agonizing reappraisal of what they missed, these women are looking at the former East German system with a mixture of anger and despair.

It's a testimony to the ingenuity of most women and to the fierceness of new mothers' love that with much juggling and concern and help from husbands and family, the majority of mothers end up with workable compromises on the question of whether and how long to stay at home with their babies. They get along with the job of raising a child, perhaps not in the way they would have hoped, but certainly well enough. They manage this task with little or no validation from our society, and often at considerable human expense.

New mothers need to realize that they are caught in an historical shift in practice and values, and that much of the turmoil they experience is a reflection of a larger problem in society as a whole. They are generally not failing or inadequate, but rather trying hard to balance their different identities against great odds.

Adjusting the motherhood mindset to the realities of working again is a major task in the third phase of the birth of a mother. Whatever necessary compromises you make will influence both your motherhood mindset and other parts of your identity. Compromise you must, but wisely, giving full weight to your baby's needs, to your financial realities, to your future as a person, but also to yourself as a mother, now and for the rest of your life.

ELEVEN

Husbands and Fathers

THROUGHOUT THIS book we have focused on the birth of a mother and the psychological territory she covers from her months of pregnancy to the reality of the baby in her arms to the months postpartum. Yet in general, at every point along the way, there is a man traveling beside her, covering his own ground on the journey to becoming a father. Although the father is an equally important figure in this drama, I have focused almost entirely on the mother's experience until now. At this point I would like to bring in the father, especially in light of how the two of you have to reinvent your marriage with the arrival of a child.

A new mother has to find a way to assimilate her motherhood identity into her marriage. It makes sense that while you as the mother are forging a new identity, your husband

is constructing his own as well—"the fatherhood mindset."
In our time and culture, the fatherhood mindset is largely
terra incognita. It's hard even to attempt a description of the
territory because young parents today live in a world where
the cultural and economic realities are rapidly shifting, and
rarely in predictable ways. Most new parents are caught
somewhere between the traditional past and an ill-defined
future. My goal here is to provide a kind of progress report
of where we are as a society, so that you as a mother can
understand some of the factors your husband has to deal
with, and thus better navigate the reinvention of your marriage to accommodate both of you.

CULTURAL BELIEFS

Couples automatically grow into fatherhood and motherhood roles, and also end up assigning specific family tasks
to each other. Consciously or unconsciously, husbands
and wives tend to work out who generally bathes the baby,
who does the laundry, who drives to pediatrician appoint-
ments, and who gets up for a night feeding. Between the
two, they not only decide who will do what but also place
different values on each task, depending upon their
lifestyle.

We call this division of roles and tasks the couple's
"parental cultural beliefs"; they can shift and change, but
they almost always fall into one of two general categories,
traditional or egalitarian. The two categories overlap on
many points, but for the sake of description, I'll treat them
as distinct.

Traditional

In a traditional arrangement, the father assumes that the mother will take full responsibility for caring for the baby. The father may partially share the work, but in his mind he is only helping his wife or easing her load, not taking it upon himself. His primary role, as he sees it, is to provide a kind of supportive network for his wife, emotionally, physically, practically, and financially, which serves as a buffer zone against the outside world and gives her room to learn how to care for the baby.

With this agenda, a father is not confronted right away with the full impact of needing to keep the baby alive, or at least not in the same way as the mother. Instead, he is hit by the sudden realization that he needs to keep this new family afloat. The impact of this reality forces him to a changed perspective on his obligations. Work and financial security take on a whole new weight. Many new fathers become suddenly preoccupied with the physical security of their surroundings, to the point of reevaluating the neighborhood in which they live, and making strong efforts to establish a safe environment for the family.

As your husband begins to shift in his self-image, he may start seriously considering life insurance, medical insurance, and job security in a way he never has before. In the traditional couple, the father turns outward to face the world, in sharp contrast to his wife, who, turning inward to face the baby, disengages from the outside world.

There are some good reasons why the traditional model has prevailed in so many cultures for most of our known history. The more obvious ones include the mother's physical relationship to the baby, which begins in her own body and then continues through breast-feeding as soon as the baby is born. From a biological point of view, it is interesting to note that the traditional model also holds true in the world of the great apes. For example, among baboons, the mother, along with her older offspring and other females, form an inner circle where they attend to the caregiving of the infant. Meanwhile, the male sits at some distance from the inner circle and looks out over the savanna, alert to both danger and potential food, facing outward and "reading" the surroundings.

No one knows whether examples from the animal kingdom are valid for humans, nor whether there are biological factors at work enforcing the traditional patterns. (It has been reported that some husbands, upon learning they are to be fathers, run around the room flexing their muscles, beating their chests, jumping from chair to chair, and whooping in their excitement!) Whatever biological factors are at work, they are eclipsed by the powerful cultural models that have been in place for centuries.

The traditional roles give rise to their own challenges. Just as you may not understand fully your husband's turning outward at this dramatic time in your lives, he may not understand your turning so forcefully toward the baby. Many new fathers watch this transformation in their wives with a mixture of confusion, jealousy, wonder, and a small sense of inadequacy that they can't enter this rich and mysterious realm of experience.

All of this is not to say that the traditional father is not interested, nor that he does not play with or physically care for the baby. He may do it all and with great pleasure, but in his thinking, his central task remains that of protecting and supporting the new family against the real and symbolic threats of the external world. One amused mother described the first indication of her husband's new mindset.

The second morning after the baby was born, when my husband came to the hospital to see us, he had a funny expression on his face. He looked sort of embarrassed, but proud just the same. He leaned over and said to me, "You'll never guess what I did last night before going to bed. I walked around the yard and pissed in all four corners, marking my territory like some dog or wolf. God knows why." I thought it was funny, but was also kind of glad that he did that, even if it was weird or a bit primitive.

In most traditional couples, the wife stays home with the baby during the day, and the father comes home from work in the evening. In this case, you can observe that his style of play will be quite different from what the mother has been doing with the baby most of the day. The father tends to play far more vigorously with the baby, throwing him or her up into the air, and making big noises. He pokes and tickles forcefully, and seems to be an expert at high-level tactile and kinesthetic stimulation. Most babies love this behavior, and look forward to it. In fact, as soon as Dad walks through the door, you can see the anticipation of a thrilling bout of excitement in the baby's body tension and face.

The mother in this case, who is the primary caregiver and is with the baby most of the day, is an expert as well, but in a much more finely regulated way that operates at lower levels of arousing the baby, and uses more verbal and gentle tactile stimulation. Before the baby's bedtime, these mothers frequently have to tell their husbands to calm down, or the baby will be too excited to sleep. Most baby observers believe that both patterns of play are valuable for the baby, each providing different experiences and teaching different things.

Surprisingly, these patterns of play are not gender-linked nor innate. When the man stays at home with the baby and is the designated caregiver, and the woman leaves home to work full time, returning at night, there is a reversal in the patterns. Then it is the father who shows the finer, more modulated pattern of stimulation and the mother who throws the baby up in the air and provides the roughhousing when she gets home.

Another characteristic of the more traditional father is that he has a smaller repertoire of games and play routines than his wife. He also has a shorter attention span or tolerance for being with the baby. In general, after he plays out his typical routines with the baby and exhausts his limited repertoire, he stops playing and hands the baby back to his wife. He then sits down to relax and read the newspaper or watch television (once again "looking over the savanna"). He turns to the outside world, where he is more comfortable.

In contrast, most mothers are far better at interactions that don't require props from the external world. They can interact for long periods of time just by using their faces and voices, or getting lost in stretches of improvised play. Fathers tend to need and use props and toys, and their play is more structured with a clear beginning and end.

If you are part of a traditional couple, it is important to realize that your husband's limited tolerance for being with and caring for the baby is not generally his personal choice, nor is it an example of passive aggression ("Look, I'm so bad at it—you had better do it"). You should not imagine that he could change if only he tried harder. In fact, this limited tolerance is deeply felt and inexplicable to the fathers themselves. After spending a period of time with the baby, they have simply had it and want to be somewhere else. After that point, if they have to remain with the baby, they may grow irritable. We know that mothers get irritated, too. The difference is that in the traditional pattern, the father passes the task to his wife, regardless of her level of irritation.

So many marital fights turn on just this point. There is the superficial issue of negotiating each instance of baby care between mother and father, and then there is the deeper issue of whether both partners have really accepted their traditional roles equally. A father's tolerance is most likely to change only if he radically alters his belief system. The acculturation that pushes boys and men to become most involved in the external world, and girls and women to be more involved in the internal world (which includes caregiving), is subtle and pervasive.

Because the traditional father is less involved in the daily care of the baby and sees himself as a secondary caregiver, he is often slower to shift his identity from being the son of his father to being the father of a son or daughter. In fact, this shift may not fully happen until the child is two or so years old. At that age, most traditional fathers assume a new kind of relationship with their child, one that is closer and more responsive. Even then, however, the father sees his responsibility less as a caregiver and more as a teacher and one who shares in the fun. In a sense, the traditional father sees himself as the one who introduces the child to the world at large, where he himself feels more expert and at ease.

This nineteenth-century view of the middle-class family structure and the parental roles within it is one that psychodynamic thinking has adhered to. In that perspective, the father's role is seen to be to pull the child out of the intimate orbit of the mother-infant relationship, beginning around the child's third year, and introduce him to the realities of society, culture, and the world. In psychodynamic terms, the child lives in a dyad (relationship of two) with its mother until the third year, when the father intrudes and turns the dyad into a triad (relationship of three). This view, however, is beginning to change within the field.

In many cases, even babies of traditional couples today are involved right away not only in a dyad with their mother but also in a dyad with their father, and then in a triad with both their mother and father. Many daily activities are now done with all three together; even if one parent is just observing, he or she is still present in the room, making a triad. For your baby, being with you while your husband is there is a different experience from being with you alone, and vice versa. Life with father no longer starts at age three for the child, but typically begins at birth, enriching the baby's experience.

In today's culture there are men who acknowledge the changes in parental roles intellectually, but still act as if child-rearing were the sole domain of the mother. In these cases, the kind of support the father offers the mother does not include becoming part of her affirming matrix. Instead of encouraging, validating, or advising from a position within the magic circle of the initiated, he gives psychological support by simply showing his love and wonder. He can admire his wife as he might admire a gifted musician, but not join in her achievements. This too can be a perfectly valid and precious form of support.

The problems arise when there is no consensus between the man and woman about the nature of the marriage and their different roles. If one thinks it's a traditional marriage but the other doesn't, the woman can end up always wanting the man to do more and share more of the responsibility. If he does not, or cannot, the mother often becomes angry and disenchanted with him not only as a father but also as a husband and a man, which obviously has lasting consequences in the marriage.

As I mentioned earlier, the point when the new mother begins to reevaluate her husband through the lens of his suitability as a father is a crucial time in the marriage, and often sets the whole future course of the relationship. Unfortunately, it is at this time that the disenchantment can set in.

Consider one mother's complaint, which is voiced in far too many relationships:

> Tom doesn't seem to understand that he has a daughter, too. I mean, it's not just my baby. He is her father, but he doesn't seem to get it. He never holds her for very long, doesn't change her, expects me to take care of her all the time, and then wonders why the house is a mess when he gets home.

Last week he started sleeping on the couch because he says he can't get enough rest with her waking up at night. What about me? I'm sorry he's sleeping in the living room, but this is a baby, for God's sake, and we're both her parents.

I no longer believe it's just about his rest. He's cutting himself out of our lives, from me and her.

This couple is moving further apart on a vital issue. It will require some work from both of them to repair it and not let it spread to other important issues that make up their marriage.

Another mother described her situation this way:

I never expected having a baby would put so much tension between my husband and me. He's not at ease about this whole thing and it scares me.

He wants me to let the baby cry and not pick him up. He's afraid of spoiling the baby. He thinks we're ready to go out again and have a baby-sitter. We fight about almost everything. He feels free to argue or criticize, but he doesn't know anything about what it takes to care for this baby. It's hard enough being a mother without having to fight uphill against him.

If I have to, I'm taking the baby and moving to my parents' for a while.

Here, too, are the beginnings of a pattern—running away from critical issues in the marriage. These kinds of conflicts can end up shaping a family's life forever. The texture of a marriage is in some jeopardy when a mother comes to the point where she declares: *I finally said to myself that I was going to have to bring up this baby alone, that this is my baby, that beginning now, it's the two of us against him.*

Said with bitterness and foreboding, this comment signals a profound rift between mother and father. This kind of conflict may lead to an enmeshed relationship between mother and daughter and in turn a more distant and difficult relationship between the daughter and her father. Years later, if the father and daughter try to draw closer, the mother can read it as treason, and the daughter may have to fight guilt. There's no question that misunderstandings about the parenting roles will cast a long shadow on the relationships in this family.

The traditional marriage may sound archaic to some, but it does have distinct advantages. When the mother and father play such divergent but complementary roles, the baby experiences a wider range of being with people who are quite different, yet intimate. Some mothers may feel that the father's contribution as part-time playmate or clown are of little value to the baby, but rather are just convenient for the husband. This underestimates the value and import of his role, which in a real sense is adding a crucial part to the mix. The traditional pattern also permits the woman to enter into an inward maternal realm for a time without interruption.

Egalitarian

A growing number of couples are egalitarian. The egalitarian couple believes in equally sharing the caregiving as well as most other domains of family life. In certain cultures and socio-economic groups, this appears to be the wave of the future.

Three major trends fuel this push toward an egalitarian marriage: (1) economic realities that require both parents to work full-time jobs to support their family, (2) the ideology of equality brought about by the feminist movement, and (3) the weakening of the extended family, which makes it necessary for the father to fill in where in-laws or siblings used to be.

In my experience, the pure egalitarian father is still more of an ideal than a reality, although many traditional fathers are being pulled in that direction. There are of course some fathers who are primary caregivers, but their numbers are not yet large. It appears that most egalitarian fathers begin under force or persuasion to take on a greater role in caring for their children, and then find that role unexpectedly gratifying. They often discover more joy in parenting than they ever expected, feel surprisingly at ease with their role, and become true converts to the idea.

Naturally, this kind of co-parenting comes with its set of challenges and difficulties as well. Sharing all the tasks of caregiving is easier said than done because many things are hard to split down the middle. Even when each parent is on duty exactly half of the time, it doesn't mean they can share each responsibility in equal parts, either practically or psychologically. It is common in these arrangements to see each of the parents begin keeping score, feeling that the other is not holding up his or her share of the workload. This can transform the arena of childrearing into a battleground.

One couple I know of went so far as to invent a system of quantifying exactly what each of them did so that it would come out evenly at the end of the week. They not only wrote down each day who swept the house, made dinner, and did the dishes but gave out points to the one who scoured the most pots and pans. Where the system fell apart was in comparing who spent more quality time with the baby. The mother described it as follows:

His idea of being with the baby is to prop her in her rocking chair while he watches TV, or move the rocking chair to the garage so he can work on one of his projects. I don't call that being with the baby, but he counts it.

At the other extreme, one parent may start to feel jealous if the other seems to be better with the baby, or enjoy him more. As one mother explained:

Recently I took a job four evenings a week to bring in some extra cash. My husband takes the baby on those evenings. I should be grateful that he is so good with her, but he gets that sweet time with her right before sleep, and she always seems to go down really well for him. Lots of nights I come home and find her asleep, still in his arms, and sometimes he's asleep too. They have this thing between them that makes me feel left out.

When parents compete for their baby, the situation starts to take on all the issues of power, dominance, and competition that normally get played out in the sexual or work arena. When these feelings enter into the caregiving sphere, the relationships of all three suffer.

A small percentage of mothers end up wishing they hadn't entered into the egalitarian bargain to begin with, and would like to see their husbands back out of the picture more and leave them to their mothering experience. The husbands in this instance feel naturally cheated and rejected. Having made the effort to arrange their lives for fatherhood, they lose out on the right to be fully gratified by their decision.

Husbands in egalitarian marriages may not be able to satisfy all the needs of their wives, and this can detract from their own gratification. For instance, a husband cannot be part of his wife's affirming matrix, which typically is made up of experienced women, both family and friends, who can offer support and advice. When a couple lives far away from family and old friends, the new mother tends to expect the husband to participate in this affirming matrix, despite the fact that, quite understandably, the new father doesn't function well in that role. While he can provide an enormous amount of practical and physical help, and can contribute a sense of solidarity, he simply is not in a position to validate, advise, or encourage as a wise counselor, which is often what the new mother needs. The fact is that he is generally as ignorant as his wife if not more so as to why the baby is crying, how to put the baby to sleep earlier, or how to make a feeding go more smoothly. He may try to help, but understandably fail, causing them to experience a sense of joint failure—almost emptiness as a couple. The tragedy is that they feel the failure is theirs, when it is circumstances that have put them in an impossible situation.

Even if a husband partially succeeds in playing the role of an affirming presence, it can lead to more complications. In the process of becoming a support figure, the husband becomes maternalized to a certain degree, which is difficult to combine with his other roles as father, husband, and caregiver. Not only are these a lot of roles for anyone to fill, but they are somewhat contradictory in character. In our society, it is difficult to be both husband and maternal at the same time, or to slip back and forth between the two. The nature of the relationship between husband and wife gets altered in the process of a husband's becoming more maternal, and it may take time for it to return to its usual state, or it may never completely return at all.

When the egalitarian arrangement goes well, however, both parents can develop a powerful feeling of solidarity. They have the pleasure of doing something together, succeeding with their baby, and deepening their relationship with each other at the same time.

For the mother who wants to return to the workplace, the egalitarian marriage arrangement has its advantages. A woman in this situation knows she can count on her husband to share the responsibilities when the time comes, which relieves some of the pressure in the first months after the baby's birth. Knowing that he will be contributing in equal measure to the household situation allows the wife to construct a future identity for herself as a mother and as a worker. She can feel that her husband truly respects this vital part of their lives together: the raising of their children. Many women in this situation feel a deep gratitude and friendship toward their husbands, which re-cements the marriage with a strong bond.

TERRA INCOGNITA

There has not yet been enough accumulated experience of these shifts in parenting patterns for us to know all the ramifications. One thing, however, is clear. The patterns are changing too rapidly for people to keep up with, often forcing arrangements onto young couples that they never wanted nor thought they would have to cope with. As a society, our ideals and theories are not in sync with the realities of our policies, placing new fathers and mothers into impossible dilemmas where there are no solutions, only compromises. Most couples find themselves inventing a string of compromises to solve their child-care needs which rarely last for a long time and need continuous monitoring.

Even the research on this subject does not yield clear understanding. Recent studies suggest that a father's identity—traditional or more egalitarian—makes little difference in his relationship with his baby. Some studies show that egalitarian fathers do not play with their infants much differently from the traditional dads, even if they spend more time on various caregiving tasks. The pattern of attachment between the baby and father appears to be the same in either case as well.

Two differences do stand out between the two different styles of fathering. Egalitarian fathers always feel that their experience of being involved in caregiving has made them better fathers than they would otherwise have been. Second, women in more egalitarian relationships appear to be more satisfied in their motherhood role in this society.

The fatherhood mindset is undergoing a rapid and sometimes tumultuous evolution, moving as a result of trial and error toward an uncertain future, pushed this way and that by influences beyond the man's control. As challenging as it is to become a mother or father in today's world, few would doubt that it is worth all the effort.

A FINAL WORD

In addition to adapting the motherhood mindset to your career and your marriage, you will have to bring many other identities into line with your new motherhood: your place in your original family, your friendships, your hobbies, and your role in both your community and the society at large. All this readjusting of your identity makes up the adaptation phase of motherhood. You will spend many years making a place in the totality of your life for this new identity, a place that allows you to flourish as a mother, and then allows that experience to enhance your life as a woman and as a person.

I have come to the end of this description of the process of becoming a mother, but the process itself never ends. A permanent part of you, it will be reworked many times over as your children grow older, leave home, get married, and have children of their own.

When women who have children are asked what they are most proud of as they look back over their lives, the vast majority, even among those who have full and exceptional careers, answer, "My children, being a mother for my children." The birth of your motherhood will inevitably result in your one day answering this question the same way.

Index